Sales Success Stories

REAL STORIES FROM REAL SELLERS

Sales Success Stories

VOL.1

REAL STORIES FROM REAL SELLERS

60 STORIES **FROM** **20** TOP 1% SALES PROFESSIONALS

SCOTT INGRAM

Published by: Top 1% Publishing, Austin, Texas
top1.fm/publishing

Cover design by: Tomsha Design
Book design by: Alex Head

ISBN: 978-0-9906059-2-8

Library of Congress Cataloging-in-Publication Data

Names: Ingram, Scott M., author.
Title: Sales success stories : 60 stories from 20 top 1% sales professionals / by Scott Ingram.
Series: Sales Success Stories.
Description: Austin, TX: Top 1% Publishing, 2018.
Identifiers: LCCN 2018910378 | ISBN 978-0-9906059-3-5 (Hardcover) | 978-0-9906059-2-8 (pbk.) | 978-0-9906059-4-2 (ebook) | 978-0-9906059-5-9 (audio)
Subjects: LCSH: Selling. | Success in business. |Executive ability--Case studies. | Leadership--Case studies. | BISAC: BUSINESS & ECONOMICS / Sales & Selling / General | BUSINESS & ECONOMICS / Personal Success
Classification: LCC HF5438.25 .I538 2018 | DDC 658.85--dc23

Sales Success Stories is available at a discount when purchased in quantity for sales promotions or corporate use. Special editions, which include personalized covers, excerpts and corporate imprints, can be created when purchased in large quantities. Send inquiries to scott@top1.fm

P092118KDP

Dedicated to the profession of sales that has given all of us so much.

With a very special thanks to those who went above and beyond with their contribution to the crowdfunding campaign that made this book possible:

Chris McNeill, Jerald Welch, Nader Shwayhat, Caitlyn Boger, M.K., Troy Odenwald, Andy Jaffke, Eduardo "Eddie" Baez, Sandra Thomas, Jeff Bajorek, Vlad Polikhun, Renee Tarrant, Kyle Porter, Todd Venable, David Scher, Lynda Dahlheimer, Aaron Johnson, Christie Walters, Greg Drose, Jim Riviello, Ron Masi, Karl Rego, Kevin Hall, Johnathan "Johnnie" Rudloff, Rachid Zidani, Colin Specter, Scott Lawrence, Dave Schwartz, Mary Jo McCarthy, Andrej Spisiak, Ernie Baer, Leila Mozaffarian, James Christman, Vito Fabiano and Ed Roberts

TABLE OF CONTENTS

FOREWORD

By Lee Bartlett

The phone rang, and a headhunter promptly introduced himself. Our paths had crossed, and we knew each other by reputation. He explained his agency had been awarded the mandate to build a world-class sales team of A-players and launch a new product line for a large enterprise. It is the same script all headhunters use—part flattery, part self-promoting, and short dialect to demonstrate they are cut from the same mold.

I was crushing it in my role and declined interest, when he unwittingly said something that caught my attention. He said the new CEO specifically told him to find someone "imbalanced."

When you have worked in the sales industry for long enough, you can appreciate the deeper connotations of this request. This leader understood the best salespeople are different. He sought to hire people with an unparalleled work ethic driven by a greater sense of purpose, because this can be harnessed. Indeed, it is a trait he likely possessed himself.

It takes many years of experience to understand the profile of a true top performer, and longer still to know how to manage them. To proactively seek imbalance meant the CEO was confident in his leadership and ability to align complex, individual personalities with the company's specific goals. This candidate profile doesn't lead to an easy life, but if you get it right, it leads to immediate market share and revenue.

Being a top salesperson is not just about customer-centricity, but also a mastery of fundamental sales skills, a commitment to continuous learning, the emotional intelligence to find opportunity in the smallest of triggers, and the ability to constantly adapt to the bigger picture. The psychometric tests used by companies to identify top performers are, in my experience, rarely accurate and therein lies the puzzle few sales leaders solve.

Scott Ingram has done something special with this book and the Sales Success Stories Podcast. He wanted to understand what makes top salespeople tick, and rather than turn to vanilla research for answers, he proceeded to interview the top 1% of salespeople in different industries. He asked the interviewees to explain, in their own words, what differentiated their results from average performers. The outcome is an unfiltered, precise interpretation from leading practitioners in their field. As you read each story in this book, try to delve deeper into the mindset of the salesperson by asking these questions:

- What drives this salesperson?
- What skills have they mastered to make the decisions they made?
- Who are they working for, the customer or themselves?
- Is their process repeatable, and if so, why?
- How did they control their emotions in each situation?

When you understand what each salesperson believes, you can replicate their mindset and approach. It will become quickly apparent that no "one thing" is happening in isolation, and you'll see patterns of behavior begin to emerge. You might also notice that certain industries suit different character traits and skill-sets. Try to separate the common and unique traits in each situation, and decide for yourself what makes these top 1% of performers consistently successful.

You will read stories from my friend, Kyle Gutzler, who describes the importance of sales momentum, and the inflection point in a previous role that led to his accelerated success. Others discuss the soft-skills employed by only the best salespeople, such as the importance of not burning bridges, courage, managing discomfort, competitiveness, and when to move on. These skills are difficult to teach in a classroom but are often differentiators that drive success.

A common theme throughout the book is salespeople referring to their mentors. The only way to lead top salespeople is to earn their respect, demonstrate integrity and remove all the obstacles to let them thrive. It is a thankless task that requires a leader to control their ego and propel the best people forward. However, as I found when referring to mentors in my book *The No.1 Best Seller*, the "thanks" comes years later, when salespeople reflect on the positive impact these mentors had on their careers. Consider each reference a homage to the crucial role these people played.

The beauty of this book is you can compare your own experiences and approach to those of the top 1% and decide what makes the difference between good and exceptional. Each story is a lesson learnt from years of trial and error. Whether cause or cash-driven, the motivational drivers of top salespeople are not important. What is important is how they align themselves with their employer and customer, and you are about to read several masterclasses in enterprise selling that will shave years off your learning curve.

I was delighted when Scott asked me to write the foreword to this book. He was the first person to read my book on the day of release. When finished, his question remains the most poignant to date. "Lee, why did you write *The No.1 Best Seller*? You didn't need to...." My answer was "I don't really know. I just wanted to tell people how I came to be a consistent top performer, and show them it is not luck." I intended to publish the book and go back to work, because I knew that past successes have no bearing on the future. I would guess the people who wrote the stories in this book feel the same. They have given something back, but they also understand it's about looking forward and continuous execution, not congratulating yourself on previous successes. The people who contributed to this book are still crushing it in their sales roles, and the next pages will tell you how and why.

INTRODUCTION

By Scott Ingram

This is a book about stories, so it only makes sense to start the introduction with the story of how this book got started.

After the first ever Sales Success Summit that featured over a dozen guests from my *Sales Success Stories* Podcast, there was a secret gathering of some key presenters (Thank you Jacquelyn, DeJuan, David, Debe, Paul, and Luke) held in order to brainstorm a collaborative book project. If you're not familiar, my *Sales Success Stories* Podcast exclusively features quota carrying, individual contributor, sales professionals who are either #1 or at least in the top 1% of their respective sales organizations. I knew I wanted to do something like this ever since my pre-interview conversation with Robbie Siegel in a Las Vegas hotel room. Here, he said that there aren't any books written by active top sales professionals because we're all too busy selling. I knew I wanted to change that and allow for a large number of top sellers to contribute to a sales book because many hands make light work.

As the group got together to discuss the book project, I asked them two questions. 'Where is the gap in the marketplace with the sales books that all of us are reading?' and 'What's the overarching umbrella, theme, and ideally working title that we can collectively bring our unique experience together into?'

Now, to be clear, I came into the discussion with a couple of ideas but wanted to see what would come out of this mastermind without too much of my own bias and preconceived notions.

As a podcaster. I have a tendency to record things and I can tell you definitively, because I just listened to the recording, that it took us less than an hour to solve these questions. The answer was so obvious that I wanted to smack myself on the forehead. First, the gap was simply that, with very few exceptions; there just aren't any real stories from real sales professionals out there (Lee Bartlett's book *The No.1 Best Seller* is one of the very few examples, which is why I asked him to write the foreword). Furthermore, why don't we just call the book "Sales Success Stories," because that's what it should be made up of? For me, the lesson here is that sometimes you're just too close to something to see the obvious answer. This is just one more reason to surround yourself with great people; ask them good questions and shut up!

We proceeded to spend the next few hours thinking about different ways we could structure the stories and the most important themes. Ultimately, we decided that the structure would probably present itself, and we didn't need to force it. Instead, we just needed to start collecting the stories and focus on assembling them later on based on themes.

Growing up, I loved reading 'Choose Your Own Adventure' books, and I think that's ultimately what we've created here. Although you'll find a high-level organization structure whereby we've grouped the stories into the broad categories: Mindset, Relationships, Sales Careers and Sales Process, you can really start anywhere you like. Most of the time, I read books straight through, and that will certainly work here, but you can just as easily skip to the section where you're currently facing a challenge or could use some advice. That will also serve as a great way to go back to a particular set of stories for future reference or just skip to a random page and start. With any luck, you're going to walk away with some great value and a great set of lessons learned.

Continuing with the 'Choose Your Own Adventure' theme, the best way to make the most of this book is to focus on "Your Own Adventure." In these pages, you're going to find a lot of different perspectives and even conflicting advice. Just like with most things in life, you have to pick and choose what's most relevant for you; whatever fits your style, your personality, and the way you sell the best. There are no right or wrong answers... only your answers.

Then, be sure to read the closing, where you'll find a specific set of suggested next actions and some ways that you can participate in the next volume of this series. Since I'm currently interviewing about 26 new top performers each year, I have to believe that this book is just the beginning and that your input is going to be significant to even better future volumes.

Here is one way you can share some great real-time feedback with us: If you read a story that is particularly impactful and meaningful to you, take a picture of yourself with the book, then post it on LinkedIn with your specific insight, making sure to tag that story's author and myself in the post. That will certainly keep us going, hopefully providing some value for your own network in the process. Thanks for sharing!

Finally, we're all really proud of this book and hope you get a lot of value from reading these pages. We're even more proud of the audiobook where all of the stories are read by that story's author, where you can hear them emphasize the key points in their own words and hear the nuances in their voice. If you've already purchased both formats, please email your receipts to scott@top1.fm and I'll send you something special. If you haven't yet purchased the audiobook, you can also email me and I'll recommend the best way to get it, as well as set you up with that special something.

The best possible outcome would be that these stories contribute in some way to your own success in sales. The results are up to you, but may these stories serve you well.

Bios

Scott Ingram

Professional history: ADP, Bazaarvoice, Eloqua, Oracle, Certain, Relationship One

Host of the *Sales Success Stories* Podcast

LinkedIn: top1.fm/LISI

Bio: Scott Ingram is the top account director at Relationship One where he works with about a dozen Fortune 500 companies to help them maximize their Oracle Marketing Cloud investments. Scott has been a part of two IPO's in his sales career having sold for Bazaarvoice and Eloqua. Scott also hosts the *Sales Success Stories* Podcast where he ONLY interviews top individual contributors who are either #1 or at least in the top 1% if they work for larger organizations like LinkedIn, Paychex, Microsoft, ADP, etc.

Fun Facts:

- Scott is married, has 2 daughters, too many cats to name (not by choice) and a Chiweenie.

- Scott is Peloton obsessed and used to teach indoor cycling classes at the Townlake YMCA in Austin where he prided himself on offering the most difficult classes available.

- Scott founded his first company, Grey Matter Technologies, when he was 20 years old. He was surprised to find the name pop up years later while binging on Breaking Bad.

Mike Dudgeon

Professional history: DDB, OMD, *Newsweek*, The *Wall Street Journal*, LinkedIn

Star of podcast episode: 1 (top1.fm/1)

LinkedIn: top1.fm/LIMD

Bio: Mike's career started in college in a small marketing department at Hoosier Down where he performed on the weekends as a horse mascot called "Hoosier Buddy." Since hanging up the horse shoes, he's hung close to marketing by working at global ad agencies (OMD, DDB) and now selling into Enterprise Technology companies. Mike is fortunate to lead some of the top talent as a Sr. Manager on LinkedIn's Key Accounts for their Marketing Solutions business.

Fun Facts:

- Mike is married with two children and a third on the way.

- Mike thought it was wise to live through a seven month renovation project and have a baby in the middle of it. His wife is not to blame.

- When not trying to setup adventures for his family, Mike enjoys mountain biking and road cycling.

Justin Bridgemohan

Professional history: BeneFACT Consulting Group, Intelex Technologies, Influitive, Total Expert

Star of podcast episode: 3 (top1.fm/3)

LinkedIn: top1.fm/LIJB

Bio: Justin has spent his entire career in software sales, and now focuses on the enterprise market. Justin honed his sales craft from the ground up; starting off cold-calling in the SMB space and eventually working his way into focusing on key accounts. Justin studied Political Science at Carleton University and Business Administration at Heriot-Watt University.

Fun Facts:

- Justin is an avid reader and typically reads 3 books per month.
- Justin has recorded an album as a musical artist.
- Justin is a huge basketball fan and has a goal to watch an NBA game in every arena.

DeJuan Brown

Professional history: Intuit, Bloomberg BNA

Star of podcast episode: 6 (top1.fm/6)

LinkedIn: top1.fm/LIDB

Bio: DeJuan has more than 15 years of experience in sales and consulting, spending the last several years serving clients in the Tax & Accounting, Corporate and Legal markets. DeJuan cut his sales teeth at Intuit, where he spent nearly 13 years across multiple business units learning the art and science of selling. DeJuan studied Psychology and Philosophy at the University of Mary Washington.

Fun Facts:

- DeJuan is the husband of one amazing wife, and father to six children, ages 4-21.

- DeJuan is a foodie whose sole purpose for travel is the exploration of new culinary experiences.

- DeJuan is an avid Crossfitter, which helps enable his love for food.

Jacquelyn Nicholson

Professional history: Johnson & Johnson, Sun Microsystems, I-Many, Gerson Lehrman Group, Percolate, Leadership X University, AlphaSense

Star of podcast episode: 8 (top1.fm/8)

LinkedIn: top1.fm/LIJN

Bio: Jacquelyn has over 25 years of experience in building and supporting the best brands in the world. Her specialties include global business development and account management including an extensive background advising and serving the life sciences and technology industries. Jacquelyn is outspoken and irreverent towards avoidable mediocrity, possessing decades of solid client relationships and expertise in building businesses in new markets from scratch. She's passionate about wine, coaching, and mentoring. Jacquelyn and her husband laugh and love their way through Sonoma county life with kids, outdoor ranch dogs, and a few bottles of wine.

Fun Facts:

- Jacquelyn is a trained sommelier, half marathoner, and avid competitive sharpshooter.

- Jacquelyn would practice constitutional law in front of the Supreme Court in another life.

- Jacquelyn is a huge fan of diabolical Sudoku puzzles and doing crossword puzzles in ink.

George Penyak

Professional history: The McClatchy Company, Raycom Media, Restaurant Technologies Inc.

Star of podcast episode: 9 (top1.fm/9)

LinkedIn: top1.fm/LIGP

Bio: George's sales career started during his college years, selling homes as a realtor to help pay for tuition. Since then George has shifted his focus to the B2B sales space. He's held various roles in including a local Sales Executive selling to small businesses, Regional Sales Manager leading a team of sales executives across the Southeast United States, and national sales positions. Today George is a National Sales Executive for Restaurant Technologies Inc. He's been an Elite President's Club performer as a sales manager and a direct contributor. George earned his Bachelor of Science degree in Hospitality Management from the University of South Carolina.

Fun Facts:

- George was an NCAA student-athlete and kicker on a minor league football team that won a national title in 2010.

- George was the youngest member of the team during his first role in sales management.

- George and his wife own a Travel Agency (Penyak Travel) that currently books over $2.5 million in travel yearly.

Debe Rapson

Professional history: Kronos, Eloqua, Silverpop, Demandbase, Sprinklr

Star of podcast episode: 11 (top1.fm/11)

LinkedIn: top1.fm/LIDR

Bio: Based in the Bay Area, Debe has over 30 years of sales experience. Her career has been focused on Advertising, Learning Management Software, and Marketing Technology. After graduating from Indiana University and an internship as a news broadcaster, she quickly pivoted to what felt natural, helping customers solve problems. She feels lucky in that she's enjoyed a rich and satisfying sales career...with more fun to come.

Fun Facts:

- Debe and her husband live in Oakland, CA with their two boys - She's mad about her guys!

- Debe loves traveling and connecting with locals, experiencing different cultures, being out of her comfort zone, getting inspired, and challenging herself.

- Favorite Quote: "What you do today is important, because you are exchanging a day of your life for it."

Kyle Gutzler

Professional history: Ecolab, PayScale, Teradata

Star of podcast episode: 14 (top1.fm/14)

LinkedIn: top1.fm/LIKG

Bio: Kyle Gutzler began his sales career in 2012 and has quickly developed a big name in the sales community. He has won a number of accolades at the companies he's worked for and set records for sales performance, along with producing popular sales content on LinkedIn, most notably, his viral article "How I Doubled My Sales in One Year." He's successfully sold across all industries, in both new business models and land-and-expand, selling to companies of all sizes, while carrying quotas as high as $21 million. Kyle moved to Silicon Valley in 2017 to work for an analytics software company called Teradata as a Senior Enterprise Account Executive.

Fun Facts:

- Kyle runs a YouTube channel (Kyle Gutzler) where he produces inspiring videos that help people navigate a more successful career.

- He hosts a virtual mastermind with a group of high performing professionals.

- Kyle's been featured by large publications such as Hubspot Sales Blog and Gong.io.

Florin Tatulea

Professional history: TD Bank, PenPal Technologies, Loopio

Star of podcast episode: 22 (top1.fm/22)

LinkedIn: top1.fm/LIFT

Bio: As a former competitive athlete in his youth, Florin's entrepreneurial mindset and ambitions have always aligned well with Sales and Business Development. Florin first began his career in sales as a 14-year old when he sold newspaper subscriptions door-to-door. After graduating with a Bachelor of Commerce from The Rotman School of Management at the University of Toronto, he worked in multiple sales-related roles at companies like TD Bank, PenPal Technologies and now Loopio.

Fun Facts:

- Florin was a former nationally ranked tennis player in Canada.
- Florin has a passion for traveling/exploring new cultures and has been to 40+ countries.
- Florin can cook up a pretty mean Pad Thai.

David Weiss

Professional history: Aramark, CareerBuilder, Hearst, Monster, ADP

Star of podcast episode: 24 (top1.fm/24)

LinkedIn: top1.fm/LIDW

Bio: David has more than 12 years of experience in sales, leadership, and consulting within the F500, and large enterprises across various market segments, including healthcare, manufacturing, oil & gas, retail, and financial services. David honed his craft at CareerBuilder (CB), Monster, and ADP. David earned his Bachelors of Science degree in Psychology from the Rochester Institute of Technology.

Fun Facts:

- David is an amateur chef, and likes spending time on weekends going to farmers markets and then recreating recipes from the world's most famous chefs.

- David is handier than he looks. He likes to try and do many tasks himself like fixing his house, his car, and in some instances, cutting his son's hair... with disastrous results.

- David's favorite holiday is the 4th of July, because he puts on a large fireworks shows for his neighbors... but secretly its because he loves to blow things up.

Trong Nguyen

Professional history: HP, IBM, Dell, Microsoft, ServiceNow

Star of podcast episodes: 25 (top1.fm/25) and 46 (top1.fm/46)

LinkedIn: top1.fm/LITN

Bio: Trong has more than twenty years of experience in sales, marketing, and consulting with the world's largest enterprises across various market segments, including healthcare, telecommunications, insurance, and financial services. Trong honed his craft at Digital Equipment Corporation (HP), IBM, Dell and Microsoft. Trong earned his Bachelor of Arts degree in Economics from Western University as well as an MBA from The University of Chicago.

Fun Facts:

- Trong is a black belt in Karate and he loves running and reading.
- Trong loves bacon more than his wife and three kids. but don't tell them that.
- Trong has written two other books about sales: *Winning the Cloud* and *Winning the Bank*.

John Hinkson

Professional history: Dan Cummins Chevrolet and Buick

Star of podcast episode: 26 (top1.fm/26)

LinkedIn: top1.fm/LIJH

Bio: John began his sales career in June of 2014. Before making the transition to sales, John had over 20 years of supervisory and management experience in manufacturing. John was a natural fit for sales due to his strong desire to help people and his commitment to customer service.

Fun Facts:

- John loves reading and spending time with his granddaughter.

- John is 100% sure that tacos are the perfect food.

- John's idea of the perfect Sunday is cooking outside and relaxing with his family and friends.

Jelle den Dunnen

Professional history: Maandag, ITERA, De Salariskamer BV, Bullhorn

Star of podcast episode: 30 (top1.fm/30)

LinkedIn: top1.fm/LIJDD

Bio: Jelle has been in new business sales for over 10 years, which is nicely split in the first 5 years at recruitment agencies and the last 5.5 years (and counting) revolved around selling software to recruitment agencies. An entrepreneurial highlight of his was being the first Mainland Europe-based sales representative at Bullhorn. Through the years he has benefitted from a wide variety of learning environments.

Fun Facts:

- He's happily engaged to Josien, his partner in crime when it comes to enjoying life and they are currently planning their wedding for fall 2019.

- Jelle loves to travel and explore, but really loves activities that involve mountains. He has been climbing since he was able to walk and started skiing when he became a teenager. There isn't a year that goes by without climbing and skiing off a mountain.

Kevin Walkup

Professional history: FleetCor, Randstad Technologies, SalesLoft

Star of podcast episode: 31 (top1.fm/31)

LinkedIn: top1.fm/LIKW

Bio: Kevin learned very early on in his life that creating win/win situations is how business should be done. Providing something of value to other people is an easy way to earn something in return. Having been in sales his entire life, he understands sales processes, the importance leveraging of your network, and how to have buyers appreciate doing business with you. Over the last 4 years, he is lucky to call SalesLoft the best place he has ever worked. He gets to do what he is passionate about every single day - helping people be better sellers.

Fun Facts:

- Kevin's first sales job wasn't selling lemonade, but selling lemons to the kids in the neighborhood that had lemonade stands.

- Kevin loves making investments that allow him to have fun. He has a collection of classic cars that he enjoys driving regularly.

- Balancing mind and body, Kevin loves to do yoga. It's his one hour per day that allows him time to find peace within himself.

Trey Simonton

Professional history: Inovis, Informatica, Dataskill, Bazaarvoice, Accruent

Star of podcast episode: 35 (top1.fm/35)

LinkedIn: top1.fm/LITS

Bio: Trey Simonton has over 20 years' experience working in sales, business development, and leadership roles at enterprise technology companies. Trey brings an advisory-style to selling that has made him a consistent top performer selling to the World's largest companies including Stanley, Black & Decker, AT&T, American Express, and GSK. In recent years Trey has discovered a passion for mentorship, coaching young sales teams on best practices and processes in order to become top performers. Trey received a B.A. in Business Administration and International Marketing from Baylor University.

Fun Facts:

- Trey is the husband of one amazing wife, and father to two beautiful children, ages 10 and 7 months that call him Obiy.

- Trey's family and children have completely changed his approach to sales and he is finding more success in his work now than ever before.

- Trey loves water sports, and when not in the office can likely be found on a boat with his family on Lake Travis in Austin, TX.

Camille Clemons

Professional history: Northern Trust, UMB Fund Services, SGG Group[*1]

Star of podcast episode: 36 (top1.fm/36)

LinkedIn: top1.fm/LICC

Bio: Camille believes it is imperative to be in a job where you find fulfill-ment. She's been in an individual contributor role for five years and has seen some success. Still, on a daily basis, she asks herself if she can do it. To date, the answer has been yes, but that is only half the story. To be in sales means something different to everyone; to Camille, it means she's able to help hundreds of thousands of people achieve financial success by serving her clients. She works in the financial services industry.

Fun Facts:

- Wife and Mom of 2.
- Former college second baseman.
- A supporter of the liberal arts.
- Paddleboarder and Peloton lover.
- Relentlessly opposed to mediocrity...reversion to the mean is for someone else.

---

* The views expressed are those of the author and not those of SGG Group

Dayna Leaman

Professional history: Wiley

Star of podcast episode: 37 (top1.fm/37)

LinkedIn: top1.fm/LIDL

Bio: Dayna has more than twenty years of experience in sales, management, and leadership in academic publishing. She is the owner of the largest territory in her division of the company. She has consistently been in the top 1% of sales at Wiley for over 15 years, was Rep of the year, and was in the top five of sales several times. Dayna was a former high school teacher and attributes much of her success to that experience. Dayna mentors, coaches and leads new Account Manager training at Wiley. She is extremely passionate about customer service and helping her faculty and students to achieve more with the noble purpose of being an advocate for education.

Fun Facts:

- Dayna loves reading, biking to dinner, and tries to do anything not to run for pleasure!

- Dayna loves fine wine and since she is a New Orleans native, great food is a given.

- Dayna is currently serving on the advisory board of the former all-girls high school she attended. She is working on a strategic five-year plan to grow and maintain excellence for the school.

Phil Terrill

Professional history: MillerCoors, The Burks Companies, Microsoft

Star of podcast episode: 39 (top1.fm/39)

LinkedIn: top1.fm/LIPT

Bio: Phil has spent the last five years focused on building! Previously spending several years on the frontlines of sales and marketing, Phil has built a grass-roots movement through the Inside Sales community. The digital enablement movement has struck the core of Microsoft Inside Sales and has piqued the interest of sales organizations around the world. Prior to Microsoft, Phil worked for The Burks Companies in Atlanta (GA), helping a family enterprise deliver facilities management solutions. He also spent time with MillerCoors, formerly the Miller Brewing Company, in Chicago (IL). Phil received his B.S. in Marketing from Tuskegee University.

Fun Facts:

- Phil enjoys traveling the world, loves tennis, and collecting vinyl. The vinyl is great, but he probably should buy a record player now, right?

- Phil is writing his first self-help book, *4Fs to Transform Life's Challenges into Massive, Powerful, Breakthroughs*

- Phil has an "artificial" shellfish allergy but cannot stop telling people he is allergic.

Paul DiVincenzo

Professional history: ADP, Cintas

Star of podcast episode: 40 (top1.fm/40)

LinkedIn: top1.fm/LIPD

Bio: Paul is a top-performing sales executive and proven closer with 20 years of experience in fast-paced business-to-business industries, including government, aerospace, general manufacturing, technology, food processing, and enterprise SaaS. Paul has succeeded in opening new markets through a successful strategy of research, identification, prospecting, and approaching new opportunities with revenue potential. Paul has been consistently ranked as a principal senior sales executive by performing in the top 5%-10% with Presidents Club and Diamond Honors at Fortune 100/500/1000 companies. Paul is currently in Global Accounts and Strategic Markets for Cintas Corporation building on success in previous sales positions with Cintas, ADP and AT&T.

Fun Facts:

- Paul grew up on an Indian Reservation in Arizona. Could be its own book!

- Paul dropped out of college to pursue a sales career. Another book!

- Paul is constantly thinking & reading about success for business, family, life...and is excited to read all the stories in this book!

AJ Brasel

Professional history: Clover Imaging

Star of podcast episode: 45 (top1.fm/45)

LinkedIn: top1.fm/LIAB

Bio: AJ started at Clover Imaging Group 6 years ago in an analyst and operations role. After two years of working behind the scenes, he moved into an inside sales role and moved to a strategic account executive role in 2016. Prior to his work at Clover, he spent two years as a high school science teacher and coach. AJ graduated from Eastern Illinois University with a Bachelor's of Science in Biology with a minor in Chemistry.

Fun Facts:

- AJ is a husband and father to an 11 month old son.

- AJ is an avid runner and weightlifter – he's run over 600 miles in the last 6 months.

- Living in Chicago, AJ is a big Green Bay Packers fan. He goes to at least one home game every year.

Mindset

1.

DITCHING THE "SALESMAN" MENTALITY

By AJ Brasel

When I first started a career in sales, I often found myself cringing a little bit whenever people asked what I did for a living. I never wanted to be considered a commission-hungry salesman that preyed on the weak to line my own pocketbook. A career in sales, in my mind, carried a "Used Car Salesmen" stigma that I found extremely unpalatable. A few months into my career, I decided to ditch the mentality of doing what was best for me and started to work on doing things that were in the best interest of my customers. Showing a true concern for the best interest of your customer's well-being helps build a relationship that has a strong foundation of trust; your customers will stop being suspicious of your intentions and will look to you as more of an advisor. The result is the same – increased compensation – but you'll end up enjoying a longer and more fulfilling career as a result. The key to gaining this mentality can be broken down into three solid fundamentals: fully understanding your customer's needs, setting realistic customer expectations and knowing when to walk away from a prospect.

Trying to plug a product or solution into a situation that it doesn't fit into might yield short-term success, but will end up causing issues in the long run. Whenever you first engage with a prospective customer, it's extremely important to ask qualifying questions and spend most of your time listening. One of the biggest pitfalls salespeople get themselves into is thinking they need to go into a call and over communicate how life-changing their product is. Forcing your way into a prospect's pocketbook by overselling does work and I've seen reps be successful doing it, but in the long run, you will kill your chances of repeat business and find yourself needing to work harder to bring in new leads. The best way to start to plant that seed of trust is to go into all calls without worrying what is going to make you the most money. Start the meeting by asking a few open-ended qualifying questions and letting your customer lead you to the sale by giving you information. If you spend your time listening to the prospect's current pain points and needs, they will tell you everything you need to know to get the sale and look like a hero in the long run. Opening a dialog will allow your prospect to be part of the buying process and will give them confidence that by going with your product or solution, they are getting the best outcome. Over time, the customer will continue to come back to you and look to you for additional solutions when needed. This is going to minimize pricing pressure from other suppliers, as well as hard feelings if something ever did go wrong in the long run.

Setting unrealistic expectations to win a deal is another tendency I commonly see in sales representatives looking to line their pockets. So many people have issues with saying "no" or explaining the limitations of their product or service. There are always nuances in business that can cause problems with a client-vendor relationship. Whether the issue lies with the product or pitfalls in the supply chain, it is extremely important to set expectations up front. This way, whenever something does go wrong, it doesn't send the entire deal into a spiral. The best sales representatives are honest with their customer and let them know of common pitfalls up front. Selling a deal with those in the open will create a longer-lasting customer relationship with that foundation being built on trust. If a customer expects flawless quality and execution, then whenever an issue arises, the representative that sold to them will undoubtedly lose all credibility in the future. Customers always appreciate honesty – if a rep sets realistic expectations, then the entire deal will be easier and the customer will feel confident communicating with the salesperson throughout the relationship.

The final and most important way to overcome the stigma of being a greedy salesperson is knowing when to walk away from a deal. If a representative follows the first two points mentioned earlier (listening to the prospect and setting realistic expectations) and the prospect's needs don't fit, it is always acceptable to walk away. Winning a deal that doesn't fit might yield immediate payment, but will cause issues and headaches in the long run. I often see salespeople win opportunities that were not a good fit, and they either lose that deal (burning a bridge in the process) or spend countless prospecting hours cleaning up a mess. Whenever I am mentoring new sales reps – this is a point I always stress. Being completely honest and upfront with a prospect, and then walking away if necessary, might build confidence that could open doors with that customer down the line whenever a different need comes up. A deal that isn't the right fit is doomed from the start and walking away from it will give you the time to focus on partnerships that are long-lasting and will yield long-term positive results.

2.

DETERMINATION AND PERSISTENCE

By Dayna Leaman

Some accounts make you wonder why you stayed in sales, let alone decided it was a good idea to start in the first place. I think many of us have these thoughts in our head at some point.

I know that more than one account brought me to this point. Maybe that's because the model for Higher Education technology sales is quite... well...crazy. For starters, the sales cycle is typically long, similar to waiting at the DMV...but longer. Many customers demand constant change, while others demand none at all. Most of all, it includes several layers of decision-makers, all of whom could undermine the process at multiple points.

Let me explain. In selling technology in education, the sales rep rarely sees the actual buyer: the student who uses the platform to study for her courses. It's an odd way to do business, but nearly every player in the market approaches it in this way. So, while the nature of the business is changing constantly, it's mainly the professor that makes the final decision about which book is being used—and if the technology is being used at all. Once the professor makes the decision, the bookstore orders the package and posts the required course materials on their website. If the stars align or the Cleveland Browns win the Super Bowl (whichever happens first), the students buy it or they purchase it directly online from the publisher or bookstore. What's more likely to happen? Students figure out how they will not use it, thereby not making the purchase and saving the money for some sort of social gathering that involves coins, plastic cups and a fermented substance made with wheat. A final alternative— the Hail Mary-- students figure out how much it's worth towards their grade, and once again ask themselves: "Is this really worth it?"

Yes, this is my fate—along with never winning the door prize at any of these company functions. However, I manage the sales process. It's a little odd, not selling directly to your customer, but there are others who do it, right? And they make money too, right? It's always been my motto to begin with the end in mind. One of my great mentors at Wiley, Bonnie Liberman, used to tell me this a lot, especially when I was frustrated or confused by this rather oxymoronic process. Case in point? My 'end' was making sure that Christine Smith at Tulane University was going to use my Financial Accounting text and learning platform, WileyPLUS. Allow me to share this story with you.

I tried for years to have Christine use my products, but she was too busy with going to school while teaching, helping her students, and keeping up with all the demands of teaching and working at a university. She always had a line of students outside her door during her office hours (many of whom, no doubt, felt that their 'C' should be upgraded to a 'B'); it was simply just hard to get to her. You'd have a better chance of meeting up with Aaron Judge after a game at Yankee Stadium. This happens a great deal in this business, but some people just don't want to change their approach or mindset. This is where fortune favors the bold.

Christine taught Intermediate Accounting for years. While we had wonderful conversations where she promised to review my products, she just never made the time or showed any real willingness to change. I got tired of waiting, so I found other "fish to fry." Nonetheless, I never forgot about Christine. I knew that whatever opportunity she might still be able to present, I had to make a number. Her business, at least for the present and immediate future, was not going to be in that number.

Then, as always in sales, something changes--something truly out of your control. Christine's father, who taught the Financial Accounting course, suddenly passed away. She then decided to take over the course.

Showing more perseverance than the coyote after falling off yet another cliff after chasing the roadrunner, I thought I saw a way in! However, there are many details I didn't initially realize; for example, she was involved with another publisher and had an agreement with them that she would use the same text her father had used.

Time passed and, as we often see in sales, time can both help and hurt. I can't tell you why I never gave up or stopped pursuing this business. Maybe it was because I liked Christine a great deal; I knew she did an excellent job in her role and truly cared about her students' success in school and their future careers. Her attitude and passion drove me to be better— helping me to think outside the box and be a more resourceful salesperson. I started getting her involved with reviewing potential projects and asking her opinions on things—even though she wasn't yet a customer.

She was getting the entire Dayna experience (sorry for referring to myself in the third person—I haven't done that since I was a pop singer). With this process and customer, I was more engaged than Elizabeth Taylor (or, for those of you who are younger, a candidate on The Bachelorette). I was beginning to understand that I was part of a special process. I was finally gaining ground, but during this time, I made sure that her feedback mattered. I had a NEW MINDSET! I had to be patient, but NOT patient, both at the same time. This is sort of like being in the front seat and back seat of a car at the same time—only a lot less dangerous!

Finally, the time had come for Christine to review a new version of our Financial Accounting book and homework system, and I was going to make sure that she did just that. I checked her teaching schedule, found her before and after class, and even walked with her to her classes. How could I make her realize that doing business with Wiley would make her life better at the end of the day? How could I do that without her thinking of me like a housefly you can't seem to swat despite your best ninja moves?

Lisa Earle McLeod asked in her book, *Selling With A Noble Purpose*: "How will this customer be different as a result of doing business with us?" How incredibly powerful. This kind of attitude can be a true game changer and force you to shift the focus to the customer. Yet, it also involves being bold. Stating you want the best for your customer and even saying it out loud is simply not enough; I had to make bold promises, share them with her, and SHOW her that I could keep them. So yes, sometimes you must be like Joe Namath after he guaranteed the Jets would beat the Colts in the Super Bowl. Who's Joe Namath? He's a quarterback from the '60s, but my brother told me that you can't talk about being bold without mentioning Broadway Joe. Whatever.

I finally called her (on her cell phone, of course) right after one of her classes (timing can be everything). I told her what I could do for her and how her life could be better---and I said it to her in a very bold tone. This is a part of the mindset. If you don't believe it, neither will your customer. I believe Yoda said that. If he didn't, it was something very close! But seriously, I told her we would take over her custom build-out and convert all her assignments from her current system to our system. We would make sure that her teaching assistants were trained on the system. We would have a student partner help students from day one, and I would come to her class and talk about the new system. Most of all, I told her I would be there for her in order to address every single doubt and question. I told her I'd have an answer and a real solution; my answers and solutions would always be centered on her success and the success of her students while doing whatever was possible to minimize the demands on her time. Once again, it's about being bold without always sounding so bold. You can call it buffering. You can call it Jedi mind tricks. Call it whatever you want, but it works.

It's human nature to get so bogged down in the process of the sale that you forget about the actual needs and mindset of your customer. This can negatively impact your morale and cause you to give up, to get sullen, to get angry, and maybe even not want to call on that customer ever again. However, forgetting that the real purpose is dangerous and that the real purpose is all about the customer and what they want to achieve. You are a part of that process. You are the driver. You are the catalyst, but you can become so focused on the task that you forget to shift your perspective and ask yourself why you're doing the task in the first place: for them.

This sales process taught me that having the right mindset is critical and that truly successful salespeople don't deal in the short term; they deal with the long term. The nitty-gritty of the process is your mindset. Your perspective. Your paradigm. Whatever you want to call it... it's what enables you to always come back to what matters—the bigger purpose and how you will make your customer's life better by doing business with them. It is SO worth it!

Lessons Learned:

- Begin with the customer's end in mind and how it looks for you.

- Find a mentor(s) and trust what they've discovered in the past to inform your motions in the future.

- Listen to your inner voice about what is working and not working—make the change.

- Don't forget the real noble purpose as to why you are helping your customer.

- Write down your purpose, prepare your own mission statement, and read it aloud every day.

3.

THE MINDSET OF
A CHAMPION

By Kyle Gutzler

After writing the viral blog post about how I doubled my sales on LinkedIn (top1.fm/2x), I also wrote another successful post which talked about a topic that is arguably more important to me than anything in sales - my mindset.

There are plenty of tips, tactics, and skills out there that will incrementally help with your sales success, but what you need to have more than anything to be a stellar sales professional is a rock-solid mindset. I came up with four keys which I'd like to unpack a bit further.

1. Why Not Me?

This is a question that I gathered from my hometown sports star, quarterback Russell Wilson. Whether or not you are a fan of Russell Wilson, you have to respect his story. He was passed up by many teams in the NFL draft as an undersized athlete that most teams didn't have faith in. He was finally selected as the 75th overall pick for the Seattle Seahawks, initially slated as a backup quarterback. He battled his way into the pre-season and eventually earned the starting spot. In just his second season in the NFL, he turned around a struggling franchise and brought his team all the way to the Super Bowl. His motto throughout the year was "why not me?" or "why not us?"

The Seahawks won that Super Bowl in a dominant fashion. I just couldn't get over this unusual, optimistic mindset that he led with. This is a mindset that I've always tried to mirror as a sales professional. I don't consider myself someone who has any superior gifts or natural talents. My advantage in sales is often in the reckless belief and faith that I can achieve greatness. In fact, at the company that I currently work for, one of my colleagues once said to me, "You probably think that you can do anything, don't you?" My answer was, and always will be, "yes." I've come to learn in my career that you will become what you believe. In the midst of a struggling season in sales, if you believe that you are incapable and that you cannot be a top sales professional, then that's what you will get. However, if you relentlessly fixate your mind on being a winner and being an elite performer, in time, that's what you will eventually become. Start thinking positive thoughts, write them down, verbalize them to others, and soon those things will begin to manifest themselves. Why not you?

2. Removing Marble

I shared a story in my post about the famous sculpture of David which was created by Michelangelo. It was said that Michelangelo described this process as simply taking away pieces of the stone that didn't resemble David. People are often curious about what you should do in sales to get better, what you should add to your process, or what prospecting tip you should try next time. However, it's equally important to address the things that you shouldn't do and what you should remove too. It's important to audit who you spend your time with as well. Are these people high performers? Are they positive and optimistic people? I've been in plenty of situations at work where I find myself hanging out with low-performers who radiate constant negativity. These people are absolutely toxic to you and you need to remove them from the rhythm of your day. It's also vital that you reflect on your own sales process. At my previous company, I spent a lot of time listening to recordings of myself. It's amazing how many quirks you will find that need adjustment. The headline here is that success in sales isn't just about addition; it's about subtraction too. Subtract the things that are holding you back from being great.

3. Patience and Persistence

I put the two of these together because you can't do one without the other and be successful. I was watching a video recently of a successful businessman named David Meltzer. To summarize his video, he was talking about how people need to look at "no" differently. He talked about how differently we would behave if we knew that behind our next 20 "nos" there was our next billion-dollar business idea. This was, of course, a radical example, but one of the big takeaways here is that people often give up too quickly. At my previous company, had I given up when the going got tough, it would have been a sad chapter for me in my career. Instead, I pushed past all the discomfort and rejection and eventually had my breakthrough which catapulted my career. However, to emphasize my original point, it's not just a game of waiting. You have to persist! Most of you know many of the fundamental keys to be successful in sales, now it's simply a matter of hammering away, over and over, until you finally break through and begin fulfilling your true potential.

4. Fire

If you've ever watched a survival show or been in a survival situation yourself, you know that fire is one of the top priorities. Fire is what makes all basic survival necessities possible. It allows you to purify water, cook food and stay warm. I think of fire as a symbol of success in my sales career. You can have all the knowledge, connections and skills imaginable, but if you don't have fire, you'll have a hard time being successful. To me, fire symbolizes a combination of passion, enthusiasm, and inspiration. What's interesting about fire is that you can have a strong flame that will eventually go out if it's not fueled with more wood. You've probably experienced this in your own life where sometimes you feel inspired and on top of the world, but as time passes, your flame begins to weaken. There are two primary things that I consistently do to spark a strong fire and also maintain the flame. First, I constantly remind myself of where I'm going by writing down my goals. If you're constantly living off the conditions of here and now, then your emotions will most certainly be a rollercoaster. Life will give you ups and downs, which is no secret. Therefore, it's human nature to react to what life is dealing you in the present moment. As a result, I try to fixate my mind on the exciting plans, goals, and dreams that I have for the future. This doesn't mean that I don't celebrate the wins that happen here and now, but if I lose out on a $500,000 deal, it's a lot easier to swallow if I've convinced myself that one day I'll close a $500,000,000 deal. Secondly, I prioritize relationships over everything. The attitude of those who you spend your time with is contagious. I know that if I manage the circle of people that I surround myself with and keep hanging out with A-players, then I'll have a much easier time sustaining my fire. In fact, I try to make it a habit of reaching out to others and encouraging my network when I myself am struggling. If I'm going through a rough season, my default reaction is to lift other people up. Helping those that I care about has always helped me, plain and simple.

Lessons Learned:

- Thoughts become things. You've probably heard this phrase before. I'm completely subscribed to this notion. I've learned that at the end of the day, I have the choice of how I think. It's been proven that what you fixate your mind on and what you believe tend to become a reality. Knowing this, I may as well be recklessly faith-filled in my abilities, my likelihood to win, and my chances of being successful.

- Don't just pile on new learnings, tactics, and methodologies. Take inventory of your behavior and figure out what things you need to cut out in order to help you be a more successful sales professional. This could be related to how you spend your time, what you say in sales meetings, or even who you surround yourself with.

- It's completely normal to face rejection and failure. Once you understand that this is part of the game, simply be persistent and stay patient and you will undoubtedly reach success.

- Consistently remind yourself of the big things that you are working toward.

- Never stop pouring into the important relationships in your life.

4.

DON'T TAKE IT PERSONALLY; THEY JUST DIDN'T WANT TO BUY FROM YOU

By David Weiss

What was I thinking? I just told my girlfriend, and future wife, that we could no longer go to her favorite Sushi restaurant—the only decent Sushi restaurant in Rochester NY—and she LOVES Sushi…She even has a song for Sushi (I will share this at the end). At this time in my career, I was working for Aramark selling uniforms and ancillary products like floor mats, bar/shop towels, etc.… It wasn't the most glamorous work, but being the eager sales person I was, I tried to sell to everyone. I was always told if someone likes you and trusts you, they will buy from you. I believed that and still do to a point. I learned quickly though that nothing was a sure thing. In my sales career, I was still very green, and took things personally. So, when I felt someone should buy from me, and they didn't, I would no longer go to their place of business. I felt as if they had personally rejected me, not my solution. Look…don't judge me; I was a silly kid back then. I am grateful my now-wife stayed with me, and she made it a very clear point that I was no longer allowed to try and sell to places she liked to go, but that is not the point of this story.

This life we have chosen, this life of sales, is ranked among the most stressful jobs you can have. It requires thick skin, grit, persistence, perseverance, and many other descriptive words that relate to mental and physical toughness. It is one of the only professions where your best day, and worst day, can be the same day.

Let's talk about that, as I have many examples of this. One that is massive and particularly sticks out in my mind is a deal I recently lost with "the largest online retailer" on the planet. This company was looking for multiple providers to help support their growth. The deal was valued well into the seven figures. It was a deal that someone could retire from. The day couldn't have been better when they told us that we were selected as a vendor they would use. They had given us the scope of work, and the final hurdle was the legal terms; legal terms we had been assured our competitors had signed, and that shouldn't be an issue. I was elated, but by that point in my career, I had learned to be cautious. Ten years ago, my younger self may have bought a new car that day expecting a win. As we went through the legal language, one term stood out to us, and it related to the liability we would hold if something went wrong. I can't share all the details here for obvious reasons, but this would be a hurdle we would not get past. I was devastated, crushed; I could see early retirement slip through my fingers. If you could imagine, this is not a company I could stop myself from doing business with. I consider that true growth. It only took ten years.

This was just another day in the life. Now these situations obviously don't happen every day, and this was a particularly bad loss, but these situations will happen. Most losses won't feel as catastrophic, but they will happen often. You will get a verbal on a deal that won't pan out. You will get to contracting and have legal issues. You will get into implementation, something will go awry, and the client will back out. There are many areas of risk in our profession (see my story on MEDDPICC to minimize this risk). It's important to know what you're getting into. If this is your life's path, be prepared for frequent ups and downs; learn not to take losses personally, and seek help...emotionally, physically, and spiritually. Maybe I'm just lucky, or maybe it's because I have a keen awareness of my shortcomings, but one thing that's helped me is that I married a psychologist. She is my rock. I have also taken up things like meditation and have a very good scotch collection. The point is, this is not a job to just go at alone. It's important to have a support structure, and a healthy one at that. You will ride a roller coaster, and just when you hit your goals, the year will reset, and the what-have-you-done-for-us-lately race begins again. If you're lucky, and have been prospecting consistently, you'll start with a good pipeline.

This is one of the most rewarding careers you can have, but with all big rewards come risks and hardship. Be ready for that, and go into this life knowing that you must mentally keep it all together. You will have bad days, really bad days, and days that will change your life in the best ways possible.

So, if you take anything away from this, marry a psychologist. If you can't do that, and if understandably so, deal with the day to day challenges you will face. Otherwise, you will never be as productive, and happy as you could be.

Oh, and were you wondering about my wife's song, it goes something like, "I want to go to the sushi bar, I want to go with you. Sushi, sushi, sushi, sushi, sushi bar. I want to go to the sushi bar…"

5.

CREATING SUCCESS WITH THE CUSTOMER FIRST

By John Hinkson

I went into car sales believing that this was the career for me. I was blessed to be able to get a position at my hometown dealership, which after being in business for 60 years, was considered a trusted institution in our community. In my first full year, I was able to set a store record by selling 501 units! I had truly found my calling; I loved what I was doing every day!

I recognized that people were starting to notice me more. Not only was I able to help my existing friends and generate new customers, but they were all sending their associates to me. I was building a great client base and those new customers kept sending me referrals. People wanted to do business with me!

Everyone was asking me how I was able to sell so many cars and the answer I gave was, "I put the customer first." This was not just a cliché to me. I wanted to make each customer feel special; I wanted to make them feel important and as though they were my only customer. Getting a new car is an important purchase and can be very stressful; for most people, their livelihood is dependent upon reliable transportation. I wanted each customer to know that this was as important to me as it was to them.

I didn't think about the money I was making. Yes, I wanted to make money, we all go to work to make money and provide for our families, but

I didn't focus on the money... I focused on giving each client an amazing experience and letting them know that I wanted to help them. My sales continued to go up, but I know it was my focus on helping people that took care of that for me.

As I kept my focus on the client first, I did make more money. My financial situation became better, so I was able to purchase the home I wanted and have nicer vehicles. However, that was not my primary focus; I focused on being thankful. I was thankful for friends and customers who trusted me enough to recommend me to other people, "Go see John Hinkson, you can trust him. He will take care of you." I was thankful to have the opportunity to work at a place that wanted to take care of the customer and give back to the community. I was thankful for my faith in God; I always remember the hard work I had put in to get to a successful place in life.

I start my day out at 4:30 am. I write in my journal and remember to thank God for all that He has done in my life. I write down my goals for the day, the week, and the year, and then I do the work to make them happen. However, most of all, I make sure I take care of people. I remember to be of service to others and I believe that everything else will work out.

- Treat every person you meet as if they are special and important, because they are.
- Focus on being thankful.
- Remember to serve and take care of others.

6.

BEING COMFORTABLE WITH THE UNCOMFORTABLE

By Dayna Leaman

Every Thursday morning, with a cup of coffee in hand and a determined heart, I would sit in my office and scan the job ads in the newspaper. Yes, the NEWSPAPER! Remember those things? For those of you that don't, it is printed in black and white; a wonderful piece of information that is printed daily! I had just left a career as a high school English teacher that I really loved and I started working as a trainer for a finance company. I was unhappy and knew I needed a change. While scanning the paper, I saw an ad for a Publisher's Representative for John Wiley & Sons Publisher that stated: Helping Techers Teach and Students Learn. That was 17 years ago, and while my title has changed to Account Manager since, I still have the same job (in many ways) and sell many of the same product lines and titles today. While much is the same in the crazy world of publishing, much has changed too. It is more bizarre, absurd, fun and challenging than ever before! My greatest lesson is *being comfortable with the uncomfortable!* The lessons have been great and very tough. The uncomfortable lesson was a tough one and sometimes very uncomfortable one to truly learn… many times, it was learned the hard way!

I have always been a "pick yourself up after falling many times" kind of person. As a kid, I worked so hard for all my grades, and while public speaking comes to me naturally now, I had a horrible stutter and was bad at math—really bad. In fact, I relished in the joy of the pain because I assumed pain was a part of the learning process of everything and even developed it as a craft. Like John Mellencamp (fill in the middle name "Cougar" for those of you that grew up in the '80s) sings in his song *Hurts So Good*: *Hurt so good; sometimes love don't feel like it should. You make it hurt so good.* I played that song in my head a lot! In fact, I naturally assumed that failure was simply a part of the process. I have always been a hard worker, did more than what was asked and with a big smile on my face, usually with a lovely sarcastic joke at the ready.

However, nothing prepared me for this job. Nothing. I had years of retail experience where I managed people, was cursed at, and worked late painting a stock room for a visit from District managers, only for them to pass through the back-stock room for literally 3 minutes or less. Retail is a wonderful preparation for a high-level sales job of any nature. I recommend that anyone and everyone should walk in the shoes of service staff and those in retail. While retail therapy is a real thing, I assure you that the therapy is ONLY present for the customer. I cherish my lessons learned with customer satisfaction and the lesson of failure and absurdity.

I spent my first two years at Wiley literally holding my breath, feeling stressed out, confused, dazed, frustrated and tired, many times being hopeless and fearful that they would fire me. Why? It was fast-paced, hard to even find and know your customers quickly, and the training program was quite literally baptism by fire. Academic publishing is a very confusing business and not your typical B2B sales role. So, the question is, 'What kept me going beyond my first year not making my numbers, and barely raising out of the ashes for the second year?' I felt lackluster and full of despair. Where did I go wrong? I was a teacher, a successful salesperson in the retail space and was a trainer—I felt like this was my place to be! Why couldn't I make this work? What was I doing wrong? I now know the answer…

I did not ask for enough help! Now, I look back and know that I did not seek help quickly enough, but remember, I thought that consistently failing was just a part of the process. However, now I was asked to meet a sales quota and it mattered—there was more pressure and more demands from managers and my customers. Also, most of all, I had something to prove to myself - that I could do this job! My boss, at the time, did not want to really hire me and it was his boss that did. He actually wanted to hire the woman who was a member of Mensa... really? I could barely pass Geometry in high school. He said I was hungry, and I was—but why couldn't I act as if I was hungry? I did give myself time. I did not ask enough questions and the bottom line is that I was not BOLD enough.

Boldness was the answer! How did I recognize it? One of my customers said to me: "This is a very hard job and I can see you will be good at it. Be patient and start being OK with the pace and the fact that this job will always be uncomfortable." Wow! That statement changed my entire attitude towards my job and how I perceived success and failure. I soon began to find mentors and I gladly sought help from the right people; to this day, many of those mentors are still present in my life. I am so grateful to those people that took the time to help me, and many of them were women. I now understand why I have a sign in my office that says: *Chicks Kick Ass.* Boy, do they! Don't get me wrong, many men at Wiley pulled me towards my success, but it was the women (who had climbed their way up and sought answers like me) that had the greatest impact on my vision of what failure means and how to be bold and own my success. Once I owned the success, I could cultivate it and keep it going! I now understand that consistent achievement is hard and so worth the very uncomfortable climb.

Today, I still own one of the largest and most successful territories in the US at Wiley for their Higher Education group, and I have grown my digital market share each year in an environment that is full of turmoil and constant change. I have been actively engaged with training and mentoring new account managers for many years and most of all, I am blessed to work for a company that listens to individual successful performers like me. I greatly understand the importance of **being comfortable with the uncomfortable** because that will never change! In fact, I am very comfortable with that fact!

Lessons Learned:

- Understand your comfort and pain levels and what they mean to you.

- Seek help; seek a mentor and/or a coach—it can save you time and money.

- Be bold in your questioning and in your pursuit of working hard for your customers.

- Take the time to help others by training and mentoring them; give your time and you will get far more back in return.

- Think about the company you work for—do they give you a purpose for your purpose?

7.

ON COMPETITIVENESS

By Justin Bridgemohan

There are certain traits that are accepted as being part of a salesperson's DNA; confidence, competitiveness and charisma are three of the most prominent that come to mind. For many people in the sales profession, these come quite naturally. You could argue that these are seen more as prerequisites rather than something that will set you apart from your peers.

Of course, there are a host of other values that you need in order to excel; integrity, resourcefulness… to name but a few.

In terms of traits that will enable your success in sales, I believe that competitiveness, confidence, and charisma can be enhanced dramatically in a short period of time while also having the most profound impact on your sales success.

After finishing school and taking my first job in sales, I approached this competitive environment with the same attitude I used in both academics and athletics prior to that; my goal was to be number one. I strived to be that ultimate competitor; the person on top of the leaderboard who elevates their performance above the people around them. The results were positive; I did well and I hit my quota. Nonetheless, I always had this lingering feeling that there was another gear I could reach.

I continued in my career for several years, always managing to elude that "next gear." Ironically, the biggest reason for this was my success. I continued to perform well, hit my numbers, and receive good employee reviews. As they say, "good is the enemy of great" and this was certainly true as it pertained to my performance. It wasn't the drive or the effort that was lacking; I wanted to be the best. I was consistently reading books, as well as seeking improvement and advice from other seasoned professionals.

With this continued passion for excellence, I had another strong year. On December 31st, I found myself at the top of the leaderboard, except that something just didn't feel right. There wasn't that visceral sense of accomplishment that should have come with that achievement.

It was in that moment I realized that all along: *I was competing against others when I should have been competing against myself. I was aiming at the wrong target.*

Competing against yourself to be your absolute best is decidedly different than competing against others. At its core, the mental approach requires a more robust level of **measurement, reflection, focus, and effort**. I found that when I competed against others, I often measured the end result and, therefore, overlooked the key activities, improvements and skill areas that needed to be emphasized in order to become exceptional.

To use an analogy: Competing against yourself is aiming to hit the ball out of the park, while competing against others is aiming to hit a home run. The end result in both situations is undoubtedly positive; however, I have found that the sense of accomplishment that comes with the former is far greater.

Measurement

With this epiphany in mind, I had to create a plan to be the best version of myself. This revolved around taking a blueprint of my current "self," both qualitatively and quantitatively. I feel like measurement is the proof of success and progress.

To measure success, I had to have a starting spot. I began by making an exhaustive list of numbers that I could attribute to my starting benchmark. I figured the more measured I was, the bigger the success I would be able to achieve. However, I would come to find out that this was not the optimal approach. After about a month of trying to keep track of all these different KPIs, I finally gave up. It was too difficult to keep track of these numerous elements; I knew I needed to pivot.

I then narrowed my focus towards two aspects: pipeline generated and revenue won. After simplifying, I found it significantly easier to focus on the improvement itself and not the process of tracking it.

From a qualitative perspective, I focused on the skills that I wanted to improve. I distilled it down into four areas; qualification, value realization, presentation & negotiation. I kept the benchmark simple: did I feel demonstrably more confident in these areas? I evaluated my skills each month. It was not the most scientific method, but the results were evident in key times. For example, I had prospects share significantly more in discovery calls, and I secured larger contracts with less discounting being necessary.

Reflection

To truly accomplish the best version of yourself, you have to be honest about where you currently stand. There were certain elements of my techniques, skills, and execution that needed improvement. Recognizing this was the first step. The second step was recognizing that the potential existed for me to be superior to the current version of myself.

The biggest impact of this self-reflection was actually in my personal life. My desire to be the best I could be manifested itself in my personal relationships as well. I sought to be the best partner, friend, brother, son, cousin etc. that I possibly could.

Evaluating where you stand as a person, as well as a sales professional, can be either weakening or empowering. It is entirely dependent on your mental approach to the situation. Recognizing room for growth doesn't mean that your current self is inadequate at all, but rather that you have the foundation to create a more powerful experience in all areas of your life. When I embraced this, I became more fulfilled, not only in my career but in my personal life as well.

Focus

As often happens, my focus in sales was divided across many areas. The key shift that accompanied this decision to compete against the best version of myself was following the 80/20 rule: identifying the 20% of my overall responsibility that would drive 80% of my results. These high-impact activities became my target and any diversion had to be assessed carefully.

The second step I took was eliminating all the noise. All the useless emails, chatter etc.- I made a conscious decision to remove these things from my workday and focus on the 20% that was most critical.

Effort

I had always believed that effort was simply a matter of willpower. While having strong willpower is a component of the effort equation, I came to believe that there is another equally important factor: a compelling, magnetic force that is pulling you towards what you want to accomplish because the achievement of it is so moving.

I had set my goal of achieving 125% of my quota for several years and I was successful in this. I realized though that this wasn't a compelling or riveting achievement. As a result, I had to set my goals differently; they couldn't just be a numerical value. My target had to be to maximize my potential as a salesperson and the feeling of knowing that I had pushed myself to the extent of my abilities - and then enhance my abilities once I had reached my prior limit. That growth in itself was the success that I was seeking and found so motivational.

With those four components guiding my mentality of self-competition; effort, focus, reflection, and measurement - I set out on a still on-going journey of being the best salesperson (and person), that I could be.

8.

ON CONFIDENCE

By Justin Bridgemohan

Being a salesperson is tough; the peaks and the valleys we experience are unlike many other professions. Our performance can be very easily quantified and our "shelf-life" can expire after a bad quarter, even after years of consistently good performance.

The variance in the economic environment, company performance, product and a whole list of other factors - is often attributed to the shaky confidence that many salespeople experience. I've always disagreed with this assertion though. A confident person should always put themselves in a situation to succeed and, therefore, shouldn't be extensively hampered by some of these other factors. If you believe in your abilities, you should be certain that you would be able to excel in a different environment - even if it means learning a new industry, having to build new connections, or getting out of your comfort zone.

At various points in my career, I found myself in new industries I was not familiar with at all. Along with learning about the product I had to sell, I had to educate myself on the market, competition, and industry-vernacular - all the while doing so in a fairly unstructured way. Despite these challenges, I've always remained confident in my abilities.

For many salespeople in these situations, they've followed the old saying that you should just "fake it 'til you make it." Alas, this has not been my experience; I always felt like confidence was not something that could be contrived.

I attribute this to my view of what inspires confidence in someone. I never believed that confidence had to be an act because its composition was something you could attain, even in a foreign environment. To me, confidence has three facets: trust, competence, and belief. Even in new positions, I've managed to retain two of those three facets right from the first day - trust and belief in myself.

Why do I attribute confidence so closely to my success in sales? Well, I've learned along the way that while decision-makers will often do business with people they like, they will often overlook those they like to do business with for the people they have confidence in. I've found this statement to be true in every industry, and in every type of deal that I've worked.

As a result, I've made establishing self-confidence as a focal point of my principles as a salesperson. I believe that self-confidence is the precursor to having others put their confidence in you.

Trust

To be confident in myself, I have found that I have to trust that I am doing everything I can to excel in the situation I find myself in. The shift for me was recognizing and implementing an internal locus of control. There is a sense of tranquility and stability that I have leaned on in order to inspire confidence in myself, especially knowing that I was giving it my all. Drawing upon this steadfast belief has empowered me to maintain my confidence, even amidst a bad quarter or losing a key deal. I realized that I had to create this internal security in myself before it was likely for others to trust and have confidence in me.

My experience has been that the catalyst for inspiring confidence in others is leading with empathy towards them. There is something very disarming about demonstrating a genuine interest in the well-being of others. This is true in both personal and professional settings. I've found that there is a sense of comfort that can be derived by making others feel like you are truly listening to them: their concerns, needs, desires, and their headspace. That comfort is the precursor to trust, while trust is the precursor to confidence.

I've found that others putting their trust in you will create a self-fulfilling cycle of confidence in yourself.

Belief

I've strived to create an internal sense of certainty in my life. I believe this is a core tenet of developing and sustaining confidence. In addition to that, this mental state of certainty has helped to keep me grounded both personally, as well as professionally. We all have been battle-tested; perhaps in different ways or degrees than others - but we have all overcome adversity, and I've always reminded myself of that. It may seem trivial, but I've discovered that the mere act of believing in myself has led to accomplishing things that would seem highly unlikely. I've even had moments where I have achieved something and I can clearly recall the moment, be it 5, 10 or sometimes even 15 years ago, where I had that ironclad belief that it would happen - and it did.

Competence

The last component of having self-confidence, and often the one that everyone naturally thinks of, is being competent. In other words, this refers to possessing the skills, experience, or knowledge in a particular area or subject.

It's true; nothing can replace putting in the work and effort to learn, improve, and ultimately develop that competence that can lead to confidence. However, many competent and even brilliant people lack confidence; therefore, they have never achieved success in the way they were capable of. I've always believed that it was the belief and trust in themselves that they were lacking. As a result, they could not inspire a sense of confidence in others and, ultimately, they did not realize their full potential.

Some of these insights I've learned about confidence seem simple and perhaps pretty obvious. Nonetheless, internalizing these beliefs and having my actions result from them is what has made the biggest difference in my life.

9.

ON CHARISMA

By Justin Bridgemohan

Charisma is a word that is thrown around often. Many think it's an innate quality – something you're naturally born with – and if you aren't part of that lucky group, then you're out of luck. While I agree that some people are naturally charismatic, I've found that focusing on two aspects that anyone can improve – your likability and your respectability – can have an immense impact on your charisma.

I think it's important to define why charisma is important in sales. I have learned that if you distill our primary responsibility as salespeople down to one thing, it would be to influence people. That is why charisma is such a powerful force; people are more easily influenced by charismatic individuals.

Early in my career, I made the mistake of thinking that charisma was predicated entirely on the eloquence of my communication. For many introverts, like myself, this perspective makes us believe we are at an acute disadvantage because of our predisposition towards reflection, rather than active discussion.

In one of these moments of reflection, I stumbled upon something. The people that had the biggest influence in my life were certainly charismatic, but not necessarily because of their superior communication skills. I was actually drawn to these people because I had two distinct feelings towards them: I both respected and liked them. However, I think these two feelings are often conflated.

When you earn someone's respect and they also like you, you have a more profound opportunity to influence them, whether it's convincing your spouse to splurge on a new TV or trying to sign a prospective client to a new deal.

The good news for me, and for many people, is that there are simple changes you can make which foster a sense of respect and likeability towards you. I have some rules that I follow to the best of my abilities in order to help cultivate each feeling in the relationships I have, both professionally and personally.

Respect

- Act with confidence, yet have an underlying sense of humility.

- Follow through on what you say and if you can't – apologize and find a way to make it right.

- Recognize your limitations – if you don't know something, it's OK to admit it yet also be resourceful enough to find the answer.

- Strive to be an expert in your domain.

- Pivot between being direct and tactful when necessary.

Likeability

- Make a conscious effort to listen more than you speak, and demonstrate that you are actively listening through brief affirmations or body gestures.

- Take a genuine interest in the other person and seek to understand their emotional state, as well as the world that creates it.

- Put someone else's needs first.

- Re-frame negative situations in the most positive way possible.

- Be consistent in your demeanor and attitude; it creates trust.

By striving to adhere to these principles, I've found that I've cultivated a greater sense of influence on the people that matter in my life. To me, that is the epitome of charisma.

10.

GIVING BACK AND GROWING

By John Hinkson

I am very thankful to have, at this point, 4 continuous years of success in the car business, and still be able to say that I love what I do. The more success I had in my career, the more I knew that I needed to give back more to others. I had always donated to schools, local groups, and nonprofits, but I have been so blessed that I felt like what I was doing just wasn't enough.

So, in April of 2018, I had an idea. I went live on Facebook and told everyone that for the month of April, I was going to donate $10 from every unit I sold to a local nonprofit. I asked all my friends and followers to comment with suggestions and help me pick the nonprofit I would give back to for that month. The response was powerful! I was flooded with suggestions for nonprofit organizations, as well as grateful comments thanking me. Out of all the comments on that post, I made a list of 70 organizations that had been suggested multiple times.

At first, it was a little overwhelming to look at the list. Some were organizations I was familiar with and some I was hearing about for the first time. I realized that there were a lot of groups in the community serving children, schools, senior citizens, and other vulnerable groups, and they really needed a lot of support. After I had been thinking for a few days about what I could do long-term to really make a difference, I received a message from a good friend saying they wanted to help. They offered to match my April donation and, as we spoke, I mentioned that

I had always wanted to start my own foundation. I told them my dream was to build something that would grow into a lasting legacy of caring for and serving others in the community who not only needed the most help but were sometimes overlooked.

To my surprise, my friend said they knew how to start a 501(c)3 nonprofit organization and were willing to do all the paperwork for me. From this simple conversation with a friend for whom I had found a vehicle a year earlier, I decided to start the "Selling Cars For a Cause Foundation, Inc." Our foundation has been able to help several organizations and programs in our community, giving back to them to help them give back to others.

The foundation has been growing and we are setting big, long-term goals to do a lot of good and give back to our community. All of this came from a career in sales, the path so many people tried to discourage me from taking, a career that has allowed me to help others, take care of my family and give back to so many. I am blessed to work for a company who constantly gives back to the community and encourages us to find a way to do so as well. We work every day to eradicate the negative stigmas associated with the car industry.

There is still a lot of work to do and it is not easy, but it is so rewarding to make a difference in people's lives. I know that all of this is possible because I had the courage to imagine a different life and I knew in my heart that a career in sales was the way for me to change my life. In doing this, I am able to help change the lives of others. I am glad that I trusted my instinct that this was the path for me, as it has allowed me to take care of others and give back to my community.

- Use your success to help others succeed.
- Look for ways you can give back to your community.
- Include others on your journey; most people want to be a part of something bigger.

11.

COURAGE DRIVES POSITIVE OUTCOMES

By Debe Rapson

Some of my most meaningful moments stem from when I've been courageous. Many of these moments are personal; for example, when I made the commitment to spend my life with my husband, or the time I chose to end an abusive friendship, or when as a child, I stood up to a bully. One can feel pride when working outside of one's comfort level to achieve what is right. This involves being courageous and working with conviction. On the other hand, courage can also yield great results in sales; it can be demoralizing to deliver a message that may not be well received by a prospect or customer, but a sincere and well-intentioned discussion or idea can create great relationships and beneficial results for both the buyer and seller. Having success in sales for over 30 years, my values are old-school and one of my touchstones is that of integrity. This is the place I come from in my interactions with people. It can be challenging when we have to speak openly and candidly with a prospect, as there is always the risk of alienating them, but honesty is what sets the most well-respected salespeople apart from the others. Most of us say what prospects want to hear, rather than what we believe is best for them, yet I insist on the good belief.

Several years ago, I was losing in an intensely competitive sales cycle. This situation began with a call that my sales development rep made to a company with whom we had no relationship, but was the genesis of an RFP process for a software solution that was pretty cutting edge in the industry. Knowing that I may not get the chance to meet the key stakeholder (let's call her Kim) again during the RFP process, I decided to make this an in-person coffee date, to set a more casual tone and to uncover the problem they were trying to solve. We eventually developed a great rapport, as Kim and I had many similarities. For example, we are both strong, outspoken women with confidence in our marketing expertise. We also share values about developing and maintaining relationships with others. During our initial discussion, Kim shared why this project was so important to their business and to her personal career. I listened to her challenges and biggest obstacles with genuine curiosity. Our conversation focused on her and that day we never discussed my solution; I just listened.

As we discussed her buying process, she revealed her key requirements, the politics, and why the initiative was important, along with her personal and professional motivations. I also learned that she had the confidence of her VP, for whom she had worked for many years at multiple companies. The VP had a different agenda; she was looking for a solution that could do much more than ours. However, the technology market hadn't yet evolved into a platform solution, and there were no companies that could accomplish all that her VP wanted in one solution. Luckily for our competitor, they had just acquired a company that was very strong in this particular function. In fact, our competitor boasted that they could do what Kim needed in order to automate operations, as well as provide the functionality that the VP desired. This competitor was certainly building a solid business case.

Kim was opinionated, process-oriented and incredibly intelligent... but she was also new to this technology and needed to figure it out pretty quickly. My edge was that she trusted me and we communicated "hand in glove" as such. I was comfortable to play the role of industry expert, sharing the good, the bad, and the ugly of these solutions.

Instead of focusing on the features that differentiated us from the competition, I honed in on her biggest challenges while keeping both of us focused on her business initiatives. However, my competitor was playing a different game. They were betting on the interests of Kim's VP and Kim's interest in pleasing her. The competition focused all of their selling efforts on her boss's interests and their solution covered off on the basics that Kim needed. Nonetheless, Kim knew that she would soon need more than the basics; she was hoping that our competitor would expand upon their recent acquisition and thus develop a more robust automation solution not too far in the future. The competition began closing in with unethical (but understandable) expensive gifts and I could see that I was losing this deal.

I received a "heads up" call from Kim when they had narrowed it down to two vendors and she shared the news that they were leaning towards my competitor. I was so disappointed to hear the news, not just because I was going to lose the deal, but because I knew that she couldn't accomplish her aggressive goals with our competitor, as they didn't offer the functionality necessary to integrate with other systems they use. Our competitor had acquired an inferior automation solution and bolted it (only with marketing jargon) to their other software, yet it was not integrated in any way and that wouldn't solve her biggest challenges. I really liked Kim and knew from my experience with her that she was not someone who would acquiesce to her boss if it was the wrong thing for the company. Kim will stand up for what she believes is the right decision, but she was being incorrectly informed and swayed by "the shiny object" that she was being told would solve both her and her VP's problems.

My concern about saying something to her was that she might shut me down or be defensive. Remember that Kim, a strong personality, is confident in her decision-making capabilities, so I had to handle this situation delicately. My goal was to look after her best interests; I was thinking about our long-term relationship, knowing that if we didn't do business this time, we would do it in the future.

Later that day, I decided to find the courage to challenge her. I called to tell her that I appreciated her call earlier that day and that I understood if she needed to go with another vendor, and then I asked her "what guided her decision making" so that I could better understand the decision. She explained that she felt she could get what she needed in the short term with our competitor, as well as the important features her VP wanted. I turned the conversation to what she had told me when we'd first met (and what I'd repeated to her many times after), how we could help her meet her initiatives, and for the first time, why our competitor was offering an inferior product than us to fit her company's needs. I explained that solving her challenges would be difficult, if not impossible to overcome with their solution, because the functionality didn't exist and wouldn't for at least the next 12 to 18 months. I stuck to my guns and delivered that message to her with a pounding heart.

Finally, I emphasized that it was important for me to tell her the truth, that even if I didn't close this deal with her, that we would work together in the future and I wouldn't be comfortable not sharing what I knew. There was silence. After a long pause, Kim thanked me. She told me I was absolutely right and that she was misled by trying to solve both problems in a half-assed way. She admitted to being influenced by our competitor's gifts. She realized that she would likely fail if she chose this vendor and she agreed to discuss it with her VP and drill more deeply into the mission-critical initiatives she needed to support. Kim trusted her relationship with her VP and would recommend a two-solution approach.

Separating oneself from the pack involves focusing on not what you want, but what's right for the prospect, even at the risk of losing the deal. It's ironic that one could lose a deal by doing what's right for the client, but that risk can be mitigated by finding the courage to empathetically communicate your reasons as to why you believe they should do business with you and by using the information you learned from them.

12.

DIFFERENTIATING YOURSELF THROUGH GOAL SETTING

By AJ Brasel

Regardless of experience, trade or position, the clear majority of sales professionals have the desire to be successful. None of us get into sales to be mediocre, but most of us don't understand what it takes to move into the top tier of our profession. The disconnect between mid-level and high performers obviously can't be boiled down to a handful of traits; however, there is a common theme. Individuals that constantly succeed in both their professional and personal life know what they want and how to get it. If you ask any high performer about the pathway to success, they will almost always have a very consistent and simple goal-setting and attainment strategy that can be broken down into easy-to-follow steps. To implement a successful goal setting strategy, any sales professional needs to set realistic and measurable goals and constantly hold themselves accountable to achieving those goals.

The biggest issue I constantly see with goal-setting among my mid-level reps is having no measurement to hold themselves accountable. At the beginning of the year, I always hear people say,

"I want to sell more this year"

What does that mean exactly? Without a measurement, there is no way to hold yourself accountable and the goal will undoubtedly fail. A great goal has a specific target that can be consistently measured.

"I want to grow my territory by 30% over last year"

All of a sudden, you have something that can be tracked. You can check back on this goal monthly and quarterly to make sure you are on track to achieve this by the end of the year. While this is a step in the right direction, there is still a massive flaw here; there is no plan associated with the completion of this goal. There is a reason that only 8% of New Year's Resolutions come to fruition – there is no concise execution plan associated with the goal. To be serious about a short or long term goal, it needs to be at the forefront of your mind daily. There need to be steps that can be taken every day that help to achieve that goal. During the achievement timeline, if adequate progress isn't being made, the plan can be adjusted to get back on track.

"I want to grow my territory by 30%, so I am going to focus on prospecting for 3 hours every day and onboarding 3 new customers a month"

Now this can easily be tracked and measured. My suggestion is to constantly be setting new goals with different timelines and track progress toward them. When I started in my professional role, I found myself getting caught up in the weeds every day. I lacked focus and was not feeling fulfilled in my career. Three years ago, I decided to make a change, and started diligently setting monthly, quarterly and annual professional goals that would help me achieve my ultimate, long-term, professional goal. I track everything in an excel spreadsheet at the beginning of each day to make sure I hold myself accountable. The desire to hit benchmarks and complete daily tasks to move closer to 100% achievement has become a game to me and a priority over almost everything else professionally. Since adopting this strategy, I have found myself often over-achieving on these goals and have covered more ground in the last three years than the rest of my career combined.

Another common pitfall with setting yearly goals is getting overwhelmed by daunting numbers. A 30% growth goal might be obtainable throughout the year, but could seem insurmountable in January. This can be further complicated whenever the inevitable bad week or month happens early on. Setting small, intermediate "stepping stone" goals is key to maintaining focus and providing positive feedback throughout the year. If we continue to use the example of a 30% growth goal, understanding your territory is necessary to set realistic intermediate goals. You might anticipate a huge Q1 due to a win at the end of the year – so you would front-load your growth goal in Q1 and Q2. If the opposite is true, you would set a modest Q1 goal to keep yourself focused throughout the year. The year is a marathon, not a sprint. Without hitting milestones and feeling successful throughout the race, you'll lose sight of what you set out for. It's also important to understand that things could change throughout the year. If an account is lost mid-year, a goal adjustment might be needed. The same could be true if you get out of the gate fast and are on pace to crush your initial goal. Goals shouldn't be static – they are dynamic and should be under constant evaluation. A goal-oriented and self-aware sales professional that goes about their business with a targeted approach is going to have a higher rate of success because they have focus.

13.

MINDSET CONSISTS OF MULTIPLE KEY FACTORS AND CAN HAVE A MASSIVE IMPACT!

By Jelle den Dunnen

The one thing that I've learned over the years and made my own is how important the right mindset is. I am not talking about the mindset of the prospect, whether they are ready to buy, but the mindset of you as a salesperson; are you ready to sell?

Focus

The right mindset will not work without having a focus, which is something that I have been taught, not something I was good at naturally. As with many sales individuals, I have the tendency to work on too many things at the same time. You cannot really excel on certain goals if you have too many different goals. Some years ago, I was managed by someone who was quite clear and direct on the need for me to focus on a few items instead of working on too many items, and it became a recurring item on our agenda until I made it my own. It was not an easy lesson for me to learn, as I suffer from a typical trait of salespeople - stubbornness.

So, if you're reading this Dave, a big thank you for your patience and perseverance in getting me to finally embrace the fact that I needed to focus and prioritize on a daily basis. It must have been as frustrating for you to keep reminding me of it as it was for me to hear you raise it continuously, haha.

I'm raising my hand for still being guilty at times to work on too many things, but hey, nobody's perfect, right?!

Setting Goals

Part of the journey of increasing my focus has been one of my favorite things in sales; setting goals for myself. I'm sure everyone in sales does this to an extent, but I'll share how I've approached & adjusted it over the years.

I'm very much a Type-A salesperson, give me a goal and I want to reach it, give me a target and I want to overachieve it, tell me a record and I want to break it, put me on a list or a competition and I want to be on top. I simply can't help it - it's who I am. Ring a bell?

If this doesn't ring a bell for you, I would suggest looking in the mirror and thinking about if you're truly enjoying sales. However, that's a whole different topic.

So lucky for us in sales, lists and competitions are typically already present within our roles, just like quarterly or annual quotas that are given to us.

Over the past couple of years, I've narrowed down my key goals into 2; personal development and an overachieving quota. Any other goals I have are part of (and subject to) the above. While both can go hand in hand quite well, they aren't always directly connected.

To set my goals, I perform data analysis on my performance to date and that of others. This way, I can determine averages, ratios, records and more to be aware of how I rank against them. It gives me a better understanding of where to improve, but more importantly, what's achievable. It's very easy to set the bar too high and you need to be careful not to disappoint yourself. There's no point in setting a goal that you can't achieve, so with regard to overachieving quota: I only work with short-term and mid-term goals, whereas personal development is easier to define with short, mid, and long-term goals.

Setting goals is something that you can do by yourself mostly. However, I've learned that discussing it with your mentors is a good idea too. I've been challenged in many ways regarding my goals, whether it was changing, refining or increasing goals, by being challenged by my mentors. The most important result is that I've developed faster than I did before, at the time when I still kept my goals to myself.

Hitting higher goals can't happen without...

Improvement. Yup, setting goals isn't enough. Despite being in sales 6+ years at the time, in 2014 I failed miserably. I set my goals like any of the years before, but while I raised my goals and the challenges I wanted to overcome that year vs. the year before, I completely forgot to be agile.

Remember that stubbornness I told you about? It was about 6 months into the year before I was willing to admit that what worked for me the year before wasn't working enough for me anymore in that year. I performed way better in H2 of that year, but I was too far behind quota to make it up in time.

So what was the end result? I missed the quota by almost 30% and I went from winning both the Sales Rep of the Year award and tickets for our Achievers Trip to an underperformer. Some say you're only as good as your last quarter, right?

Anyway; That was NEVER EVER going to happen to me again.

I went to the Achiever's trip 3 out of 3 times since and won the Sales Rep of the year the last 2 consecutive years in a row, but sometimes a colleague or manager still refers to it as "... a certainty for the Achievers Trip and hitting quota, but there was this one year..." It's a big flaw on a great streak, and it stings!

Lesson learned, keeping agile and improving yourself is super important. I'm reviewing all my goals as part of the QBR prep that I need to do anyway since a part of my goals are attached to quarterly reviews that I have with my team on bookings and other performances. However, my short-term goals are something that I review at least every other week as I need to keep them at the top of my mind and keep working on them.

Buddying up is another thing that I learned to value a lot on this matter. You need someone to keep you honest, provide constructive feedback and, quite frankly, call you out on your bullshit. To me, that has been my fiancée for several years; whenever my narcissistic side gets the better of me, she tells me off, but she's also the same person to talk me up when I've been battered with challenges or obstacles. People mostly remember how loud we are when we win a deal, but they often forget that we take a whole lot of beating along the way, often happening in procurement, both internal and external.

Having support at home is important; it is also very important to have a true buddy at work that you discuss your goals with, that knows your work environment, the working language, deals you're working on and, of course, FFS, who knows all the TLAs that we use in a business conversation nowadays.

Continuously being focused on improving, no matter how small the improvement is, is something that we as salespeople can learn from top athletes.

Belief & Confidence

As I've eluded to already, confidence and believing in yourself are both super important. It still surprises me regularly that many salespeople are trying to sell something while they aren't 100% convinced of their ability to sell that specific product or service, typically followed by complaining with the usual arguments about why this service or product 'isn't ready to be sold' yet or 'difficult to sell.' If you don't believe in it yourself, it's most likely not going to happen in the first place.

This is something that can be very confronting and it is the same confrontation that the younger me had to go through as well. I found it difficult to sell certain products or services because I didn't believe in them, or sometimes because I didn't believe in my ability to convince the customer of the tougher sell. Some products or services are simply more difficult to sell, but there shouldn't be a reason not to try without giving it your very best. That also includes being confident that you are going to sell it, and if it's unsuccessful, you can only learn if you fail, right?

As Edison said: "I haven't failed 1,000 times. I have successfully discovered 1,000 ways to NOT make a light bulb."

My analysis showed me that I was selling a subset of our products, and that impacted the total deal value. My focus at the time was on my goal to increase my average deal value, so I had to change my game to be able to achieve my goal.

I went through the experience several times through the years when I realized I had to make a change; at those exact moments, I made the decision to sell those products from there on out. I chose to alter my mindset, which became 'I am selling you XY+Z' and it replaced my mindset of I am just selling X and Y because that was the easy sell. When I changed my mindset about the product suite I was selling, I actually sold them from that moment on!

The lack of sales on those products and services wasn't impacted that much by the quality of the product/service itself or the needs of the client (assuming we've done proper deal qualification); it was mostly impacted by changing my own mindset.

Mindset

Defining your mindset.

Focus.

Prioritize.

Analyze where to improve.

Set your goals.

Define your mindset.

Break your comp plan.

I've eluded to several goals already, but let me share some other examples of how I work with the right mindset today.

Going to the Achievers Trip. I'm sending out a PTO request the moment the location and dates are known of next year's achievers trip, which typically is about 7 months prior to when the results are in and about 10 months before the actual trip takes place. In other words, there are still hints of my sunglasses in my tan from the previous Achievers trip while sending out the PTO request for next year's trip.

Also, when I open up my browser it opens up with 3 items; my e-mail, my to-do list (which includes my short-term goals) and 3rd; the website of next year's Achievers Trip location.

Achieving quotas. Don't set a goal of hitting quota; set a goal to become #1.

Hitting your goal should be a given. There should NOT be a scenario in your head where you're not hitting your quota. The variable isn't if you are going to hit your quota or not, but by *how much* you are going to overachieve your quota.

Increasing your performance. It's not a question of whether or not you are going to increase your win rate; it's a question of by how much you are going to increase your win rate. The same applies to any other goals you might have; increasing your deal value, decreasing your discounting levels or decreasing your average time to close... and the list continues.

A more day-to-day example of mindset is deal strategy, but that will follow in my *Deal Qualification* story.

Relationships

14.

I'M 6'4" AND DEVILISHLY HANDSOME

By Trong Nguyen

When you talk to sales managers or the VPs of Sales, they always ask the same questions: "Do you have relationships with the CXO? What's your relationship with the CXO? How can you close that deal without the CXO's support?"

These questions are not in the wrong; I just don't think they're very helpful. If they just pivot a little bit, the whole conversation changes. What I would ask is: "How can we develop relationships with the CXO?" When you start asking that question, it inevitably lends itself to deeper thought and introspection.

Most sales reps take a very binary approach to relationships – they are on or off. They either have these relationships or they don't, at least in their minds. Invariably this perspective leads them down a linear approach to addressing the issue at hand. If they don't have a relationship with the CXO, then they go out of their way to build that relationship directly. They invite the CXO to social events, dinners, and whatever else they can in the hopes that these bonding moments will lead to future sales.

Direct strategies are useful in certain situations, but not all of them. I would submit that there may be a better way to build these executive relationships. Instead of going at it head-on, I want to provide you with a framework in which to think about how you can develop and influence your relationships. This framework is applicable in your personal life as well as your business life. It's applicable whether you are a customer-facing sales representative or if your work function is internal facing.

In the 1960s, industrial psychologists David Merrill and Roger Reid did an extensive study around dimensions of assertiveness and responsiveness. From that study, they came up with a 2x2 matrix outlining four social styles: analytical, driving, expressive, and amiable. When I first read the study, I wept for days; I was overcome with joy. Forget SpaceX or Tesla, this revelation was akin to Elon Musk harnessing his brilliance in physics and engineering to find a way of creating hickory smoked bacon out of thin air.

Here's the practical application of this theory:

1. **Step 1:** Perform a personality analysis on the CXO, senior executive, or any person you want to build a relationship with, and then place them in one of the four quadrants.

2. **Step 2:** Then, look at all of the people that influence that person. Perform a personality analysis on those people and place them into the appropriate quadrants.

3. **Step 3:** Now think about all of the people that influence the people that influence the client. Do a personality analysis on those people and place them into the right quadrants.

4. **Step 4:** Complete a relationship alignment exercise. Find the right people in your organization to connect to all of those people you have identified and start building up those relationships.

Here is the execution of the process in its visual form.

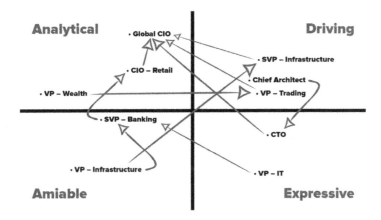

Over time, what you have essentially done is executed a complete surround strategy. The main reason why this strategy works is that you are not dependent on one person for success or failure. In our highly matrixed world, decisions are made by committees or groups of people. That's why this strategy has been so successful over time.

I was working with a global manufacturing company based in Chicago and I executed this strategy to build the right relationships with the Global CIO. Along the way, I had built relationships with the VP of Architecture, SVP of Operations, SVP of Infrastructure, etc. It took me six months and I hadn't spent any time with the Global CIO at all. Instead of shooting for the moon right away, I first built a ladder to the clouds.

By now I had solved numerous complex issues for this company and had built up my brand as a creative problem solver and Mr. Fixit. It didn't matter if you had hardware issues, software issues, or more. With some duct tape, vinegar, and a pair of chopsticks, I could make MacGyver look bad. I completely influenced those who would influence the Global CIO.

With my reputation now in the bag, I asked the Chief Technology Officer to introduce me to the Global CIO. When I went to the meeting, she said something to me that I will never forget. She said, "Trong, after all of the great stories I had heard about you, I just pictured you would be 6'4" and devilishly handsome."

I told her I was! It was the start of an enduring and beneficial relationship.

Lessons Learned:

- Developing senior executive relationships takes time. Focus on strategies that develop these long-term relationships. Like all relationships, trust is earned, and it is earned over time.

- If an executive tells you how powerful they are in the company, they aren't. The only ones that tell you that are the insecure ones who aren't the real decision makers. Einstein didn't have to go around telling people how smart he was - you just knew.

- Be genuine and authentic. Smart people will see right through people who aren't genuine. If you don't like sports, don't pretend to be a sports fan just to impress a customer. Find some other common ground to build the relationship on.

- Influence those who would influence the relationships you want to develop.

- Perform a personality analysis to understand the person you want to develop a relationship with so that you understand their motivations and what makes them "tick."

- Use multiple approaches for building relationships. These include direct, indirect, and surround strategies.

- Focus on adding value, as that will be the foundation for long-term relationships.

- Network and build relationships well before you need them. When the time comes, they will be more open to helping you.

- Integrity is non-negotiable; work only with people of integrity. Steer clear of those people who are morally ambiguous.

- Leadership styles and approaches change over time. A leader who was good for a particular time and situation may not be suited to other circumstances.

15.

BUILD RAPPORT

By Jacquelyn Nicholson

One thing I've always been particularly passionate about is getting to know the organization to which I need to sell. It's absolutely critical in complex enterprise sales and, frankly, quite helpful in almost any situation. It starts with getting to know the people there, especially the ones responsible for making the decisions, of course. You see, research on the company, the industry, and any market factors will only take you so far; you need information on a company's decision-making process, buying criteria, money, timing, power, and much more. Getting this information isn't always easy. In order to even start doing so, the first step in trying to get information from someone is establishing some level of relationship and some form of trust. That all begins by building rapport.

Rapport is defined quite easily and is considered "a relation or a connection, especially a harmonious or sympathetic one." As you can see, establishing this with a prospective customer would be very beneficial.

In 2016, I was in the earliest stages of a deal cycle with the marketing department of a large financial services institution. I was trying to close the business to help them revamp their entire approach. As a part of the process, I was invited to participate in their internal sales gathering to hear the new CMO speak and possibly get to meet him. Before hearing him speak, the person who had invited me noticed that he was nearby, outside of the room he'd be speaking in, and he was standing in a circle surrounded by a group of suits. This CMO was my companion's new boss, and she decided we should go say hello.

We approached this large circle of people and, upon introductions, it was apparent to me that the lot of them were in danger of appearing like sycophants. I was determined not to do the same, but I nonetheless needed to make sure I somehow connected with him in this odd circumstance. My companion introduced me during a lull in the conversation, and I observed that he had what seemed to me to be a Scottish accent.

I asked him something about it, and he confirmed he was a Scot and told me that this meant a few things - his words not mine! - that he was in a perpetually bad mood, was very direct, and was a pain to work with. We laughed quite a bit.

I don't remember what the circle was doing. I do remember distinctly, however, that he treated me differently, more jovially, after that. So instead of sucking up to him like I imagined the suits might have done, I then related a fun story from my travels in working with one of my customers who became a friend over the years, who was also Scottish. I told him one of my favorite stories, which involved this friend making recommendations for Scotch whisky purchases for my husband.

The CMO was amused by my whisky-buying story and my trouble with understanding my friend at times. Next, he asked about my family and this led to me talking about football and my son. He asked me if I meant American football and I told him in no uncertain terms that I did not. I asked him who his team was and he related that it was Liverpool; I shared that mine was Real Madrid. Now, suddenly in my mind, I have a perfect opening to tell him how much I loved the announcer on BEIN sports, Ray Hudson, mostly because at the time I mistakenly believed that Hudson was a Scot as well.

Although it seems crazy now when I write it down, at the time, it just seemed somehow normal, as I was just doing what I naturally do. I proceeded to do my best impersonation of Ray Hudson, with the full-on brogue I know and love. Afterward, the CMO was laughing at me while I was saying, "Well, hey, I didn't do a half-bad job of imitating this semi-famous and hilarious man for his over the top analogies while commentating!" He basically told me, "Yep, but he's a Geordie!" We laughed and laughed. This sparked more conversation and some pleasant banter about teams and his perpetual disappointment with Liverpool (no longer true in 2018!) While I learned something new about Hudson, I'd also formed a bond with the CMO too.

In the upcoming weeks, I was able to message him about Liverpool and other things, and in the end, closed a deal worth over $1.5M in a matter of weeks, instead of the traditional months. I believe that the friendship we started in that lobby over laughter, soccer, and Scottish stories earned me the right to visit their offices many times, accelerated the negotiations, eased the legal process, and enabled my company to become a trusted partner. This was all because I wasn't going to join the usual circle of chatty suits but rather was interested in having a real conversation.

16.

MY DAD WAS RIGHT!

By Dayna Leaman

When you drive up to your home, do you get excited (or not excited) to see the car of a friend, loved one, or spouse? I know—a strange question as to how this would relate to sales, but it does. It is a real raw, heartfelt emotion about the way we FEEL instantly; the way we react to what we know to be TRUE inside of ourselves. This raw emotion is exactly how our customers feel about doing business with us. It's true and it's powerful!

Dianna Maul and Janelle Barlow talk about this idea extensively in their book, *Emotional Value: Creating Strong Bonds with Your Customers*. In their preface, they state: "By understanding the critical role of emotions, organizations can take their customer's offerings to new levels of refinement, compete more effectively, and most importantly, better retain both customers and staff." This is so simple, yet many of us forget to think of sales in an emotionally intelligent manner. Think about this—when you go to a local restaurant: would you go back if the service was not good and you did not feel that you were being treated right (even if the food was amazing)? Some people do, but most people I know would not! I live in the food capital of the world, New Orleans, and I can tell you-no matter how much food matters, service matters just as much or even more. This is exactly how our customers feel and think. I have learned that understanding the connection I have with my customers is vital and the way they feel about me and vice-versa is so important in order to establish, cultivate, and expand the working relationship I hope to have for a long time.

I have been lucky enough to work with many of my customers for over 17 years. This is a true blessing and a gift; I have worked hard to cultivate these relationships with the understanding that they could leave at any time. Yes, they could leave me—customers can take your long-standing relationship for granted; this is happening in your world of fast-paced technology and offerings for the promise of more and better prices. Business is business in the end, but I do take it to another level of being personal because if I do, I will put myself on the line for my customers with my company. This can make all the difference in the way I fight for them and they know that! So, how do you cultivate this? I constantly ask myself this question: "How would they feel about their experience with my company today, and how can I help them *better* today?" I create plans around this philosophy and always look internally to delight and impress my customers. I have created a large sticky note in my office that states:

"How will this customer be different as a result of doing business with us?"

A long-time customer of mine at a university got the opportunity to meet the author of one of the titles I sell. He could be very abrasive and hard at times, even with me- and I know he liked me a great deal; otherwise, I would not have had the business for over 15 years. He told my author: "You know your book is OK, you are a talented writer, but the only reason we stay with your book is Dayna and once she leaves Wiley, we will be done with your book." This shocked me and, while it made me feel good, it was a bit odd, as I did not want my author to feel hurt or embarrassed. I asked the professor why he said that him. He replied: "It is true Dayna, because in the end, that relationship we have with you is the important one—you are one that shows up; we use his book and his resources, but you are the one that supports us and our students. You are what matters most." Now I look back and I know that if he could see me drive up to his building at school, he would be happy that I was there. That is powerful!

So how do you develop the emotional personal relationship effectively? By doing it—by listening to your customers, looking them in the eyes and using your emotional intelligence to read them and understand their inner motivation and why they want to do business with you, not just your company. This takes time to study and learn. You must do your homework on their prior experiences with companies and the people they have worked with over the past few years.

Over the years, I created a top 10 list of questions that revolve around the customers' feelings and experiences, and I constantly ask those questions time and time again until I know them by heart, or they simply become just a natural part of the conversation. I then take the information I gather and build a customer service plan for that customer based on their critical needs in alignment with their emotional needs and their goals.

People will not partner with people they don't understand and/or like! When you start with the heart's purpose and understand their feelings, you can show up as your best self to your customers - they can see it and feel it. Needless to say, this intensifies your empathy and assertiveness.

My best and most loyal customers know that I have their strategic goals in mind and I know I understand the emotions behind their goals. Many of my customers in Higher Education are constantly working hard towards gaining tenure at their institutions. So, I keep that in mind. One young professor told me early on in my career: "Dayna I don't care about this right now; I can't; I don't have time and I can't do it all." I told him: "Please, I care very much; let me care for you so you can do what you need to do to get tenure." Getting tenure is like being a Supreme Court judge— a lifetime appointment. So, they don't have time to plan their syllabus, pay attention to students and create their own resources---this is where I come in with my products and services. Their heart and all their emotions are all in getting tenure—it is their life! When I keep their goal of tenure in my mind and help them achieve their goals, they are very faithful to me and to Wiley. In the end, I can care for them and I am happy to because the customers will always remember this. What may be important to you may not always be the most important to them, and I remind myself of this every day.

My customers know that I will go to the ends of the earth for them. That is powerful. It has served me well for many years of constant success. It does not necessarily mean that things will always go right; I have failed and made the wrong moves, but none of them were a misstep as such for the customer. There were many times that I could not make something happen and I always apologized on behalf of my company, even if it was not my own fault. In fact, my biggest challenge was just that—having to sincerely apologize for selling a platform that simply did not work and perform as promised. I did a massive apology tour, talking to every customer and making sure they knew that we could and would be better. They all stood by me and that year I was still Rep of the Year—it was an amazing testimony to the power of solid relationships and, yes, being liked. I knew that people stood by me no matter what, and I knew what I would do to help support them and make sure this never happened again.

My father always told me these three things about building strong customer relationships:

BE LIKED

BE KNOWN

KNOW WHAT YOU ARE DOING

I have always held this advice close to my heart and it is so very true! I know I provide real value to my customers because I work hard, I listen, and I truly *care* for them as people. In this world, it is so easy to not get out of your head and listen and see your customers as real people who have feelings, emotions and challenges. I believe that when my customers see my proverbial car in their driveway, they get excited. I know that I do!

Lessons Learned:

- Understand and learn emotional intelligence for yourself and your customers.

- Take time to learn your customers' world and what truly matters to them—stop and listen carefully.

- Create a top 10 list of questions that matter to your customer to make sure you are getting to their goals.

- Your customers' goals may not fall in line with your goals—make them align by addressing their need and care for them! They will let you!

- Challenges, missteps, and mistakes can help strengthen the bonds between you and your customers.

- Be liked, be known, and know what you are doing; in that order. My Dad was right!

- Pay attention to your emotions; they drive your customers' goals and influence your sales.

17.

PEOPLE TO PEOPLE SALES

By Paul DiVincenzo

Being successful in sales really should not be hard... Most books and theories I have seen love to over-complicate and create many technical frameworks around sales. However, almost all of them are highly valuable and great tools to keep yourself motivated to push forward and become better as a sales professional. It's great to hear annual updates and new ways to communicate and market to people. I endorse many of them and utilize them on a day-to-day basis; nevertheless, the cornerstone of sales success will always be the people.

At this point, I have been in sales for 20 years. I started when I was 19 years old after reading the book *Selling For Dummies* written by Tom Hopkins. After reading Tom Hopkins' story, I decided to follow in his footsteps and get my real estate license to sell my way out of my lower blue-collar background. I studied hard for two weeks by locking myself in the house and reading books 3 inches thick to study for the state exam in California. I took a crash course at a real estate firm, studied overnight, and drove to San Diego California at six in the morning to take my real estate exam. Everyone said most people take it a few times, but I passed on the first try! I found some small success quickly in real estate. I went to work for a company called First Team Real Estate and sold my one and only real estate sale to Mark Kozak, the prior marketing manager for Entrepreneur Magazine in Orange County, California, when I was just 19 years old. Little did I know at the time that I had uncovered a key component to sales success that I have since forgotten about and come back to many times throughout my career. On my first day at the real estate office, I was handed a list of potential clients that had called into the firm and I proceeded to cold call them every evening to set appointments. I was setting appointments with potential buyers to present our firm and why they should sign an exclusive agent agreement with me, a 19-year-old kid, and not shop around with every agent in the marketplace.

One night, I secured a meeting with Mark and his wife for me to present to them. I was so nervous that I completely forgot my whole script and <u>simply talked with them</u> about their career, family, and what the house would mean to them. I nervously asked them for the exclusive rights to help them find this home and started to blurt out why they should go with me versus signing with a more experienced agent. Mark told me they were going with me because of our conversation and their belief that I wasn't a salesperson like many of the agents they'd met. Of course, I was ecstatic and completely unprepared. I had already run out of money and real estate is a 100% commission job. I had to take a side sales job at a cellular phone company to make some money for gas to continue to hunt and find a home for Mark. Ultimately, I was successful in finding that house and closing that one real estate transaction; however, I was unprepared for the financial hit that it had taken for me to get there. I decided I'd have to put my real estate dream on hold to focus on what could be a promising corporate sales position.

My cellular phone sales career took off from that point and I was in business to consumer sales. After about a year, I moved over to corporate wireless sales with AT&T and had a multi-year Presidents Club selling career at the company. When I moved to AT&T, they had a great training program. I learned all about question-based selling and the 10-step selling process for wireless sales. We had the training, scripts, role plays, leaderboards, trackers, KPIs, and all the other trappings of a traditional sales environment. It was exciting and technical, but I absorbed every piece of it. However, my first three months at AT&T were a disaster. I had a horrible first quarter at AT&T corporate and my manager was subsequently questioning his hiring decision. I wondered what had happened, as I felt more empowered than ever with all the sales tools and tactics. I thought back to why I was able to win Mark over versus any other agent he could've gone with. I realized that *I must truly engage people in each encounter* and my product or solution knowledge would be self-evident. The next quarter, I was number one in the western region and continued to be one of the top sellers for three years running after that with AT&T in the Western Group. It can take serious effort to not let your training, quota, personal situations or any other stress be in your mind at the time you are selling. *The secret was to focus on the person in front of me... and nothing else.*

I have now been to the Presidents Club and Diamond Level over 13 times across two Fortune 500 companies, selling upwards of 13 million dollars in contracted revenue in my best year. The interesting part of my sales career in the corporate environment, whether business to business, business to consumer, or real estate, has been the fact that my success in any sales engagement was dependent on how I engaged with the person in front of me. It simply IS the difference to winning consistently over time. In other words, I have focused on *them* and truly have come to know them at all levels of a professional sale. This may sound obvious, but when you have KPIs, quotas, increased projections and managers asking for more numbers, along with everything else in life coming at you at the same time, it's easy to get buried in a technical sales process, follow the 10 steps, remember your objection handling etc. Most of the time when you do this you will look back on how you lost and it will be because you didn't focus on the people. The reality of sales success long-term is how positively engaged you are and how much you can get the person you're selling to engage with you. It doesn't mean that you shouldn't know your product and be an expert in it to provide value. However, many times YOU are the difference to the customer. They can buy many other products and services that are going to be similar to what you're offering, and *how* you engage with that prospect is going to be more important than all your features and benefits.

Lessons Learned:

- Focus on the person you are selling to.

- Clear your mind of hurdles in your life or your KPIs while truly trying to engage someone.

- Inject enough of your true personality into the sale at all times to ensure consistent sales success.

- KNOW THAT YOU ARE THE REASON MANY PEOPLE WILL BUY FROM YOU.

- Don't be lazy, of course:

    - Prepare yourself and be an expert.

    - Know your business, sales process, and competition, and have the ability to articulate your value.

18.

THE PLAYA

By Trong Nguyen

I was holding hands with my girlfriend Natalie. As we were walking through Western University's beautiful campus, my hands went clammy. I was in my last year as an undergrad and our relationship had progressed to that awkward point at which you start to ask the hard questions. Some questions you don't ask—mainly because you aren't ready for the answers. As I got ready to speak, I could feel my heart pounding in my chest. God, I was nervous.

"Natalie, I have to tell you something."

She squeezed hands and looked at me with bright brown eyes that could melt icebergs.

"I have an interview in two weeks with a computer company in Toronto." I figured that this would be the beginning of the end of our relationship. I was moving on. She had another year left at Western. Long distance relationships never work. Shoot, I was a playa before they even invented the word.

"Trong, that's awesome. I'll come with you!"

Damn. I was definitely wrong. The only playa in my dorm room was the cassette playa that my parents gave me in ninth grade. Over the next two weeks, I diligently prepared for the interviews. Natalie helped me refine my style, answers, and how I came across. I felt confident. I felt good. I was Rocky Balboa running up the 72 steps up to the Philadelphia Museum of Art.

I breezed through the first three interviews. They had three different sales managers poke me with three different criteria that were important to the company. I saw the questions coming from a mile away and hit each one of them out of the park. I was hot. I was on fire. One more interview to go and I was done.

My last interview was with Peter. Peter was the VP of Sales. He would be my ultimate boss. If I couldn't win him over, it would all be over. When I did my research, I found out that in his prior role, Peter was also the VP of HR and had been in HR for a long time. If he was the VP of HR, then what he specialized in was people. As a result, he would see through me in a nanosecond. My hands started to get clammy and my heart pounded in my chest, reminiscent of my conversation with Natalie.

What had I learned from that conversation again? The only playa in my dorm room was my cassette playa. Bingo. As Peter asked me the questions about why I wanted to go into sales at the company, I decided to drop the facade and just be myself **(Authentic)**. I told him that I grew up dirt poor. I needed to make a lot of money to support my family and live the lifestyle that I wanted to live **(Long Term Perspective)**. I told Peter that the business I started in University was a complete failure **(Honesty)** and I didn't make the kind of money I needed in order to pay for this year's tuition. I told Peter that I was going to blow out my numbers for him because failure was not an option. I left everything on the field. If I didn't get the job, then it just wasn't meant to be. Peter told me that someone would get back to me in two weeks.

Over the last two decades, I've had the pleasure of working with so many talented procurement professionals. Some of those relationships were uneventful and some of those partnerships were also unmitigated successes that I will never forget. What made the difference between those two experiences? From a sales rep perspective, what makes for a great procurement person? What qualities or attributes do sales reps value the most when they are dealing with procurement professionals?

I've thought about it long and hard and I want to share some of my personal thoughts on what qualities and traits I value in a procurement professional. Here goes:

1. **Integrity/Honesty:** This is definitely one of the top qualities, if not the top quality I look for in a partnership or relationship. I cringe when procurement professionals don't have integrity and honesty. Let's be candid. We've all been there. We've been in sales situations or negotiations where the procurement person we are dealing with will blatantly lie to us in order to get a better deal or use us as cannon fodder for a decision that they have already made but aren't honest enough to express. What about the times when we need to get a deal done and the procurement professional tells us that if we give them A, B, and C, they'll get the deal done? We give them those things and sometimes the deal still doesn't get done regardless.

2. **Long-Term Perspective:** I really value procurement professionals who want to see things from a long-term perspective; they want to build relationships and make sure that their company is getting the best deal for the long term. They aren't there just to negotiate the best immediate deal, collect their bonus, and move on. In these types of relationships, the procurement professionals don't really care if the vendor bleeds on the deal or not; they only care about getting the best deal for their company. As a result, these relationships are not sustainable for the long term.

3. **Authentic:** A lot of procurement professionals I deal with put this wall up around them. They hide behind a facade of professionalism and distance. While professional, their interactions have a hint of contempt and lack of respect for salespeople. I always find this to be unfortunate, as I am not sure that it is the most productive way to deal with others. When you take a step back, we are all just people. We are there to do a job (and we want to do it well) but we all have personal lives and interests that make us people. The faster we relate and deal with each other as people, the better the relationships we will form. The better the relationships we have, the more we go out of our way to make each

other successful. That is truly the mark of a good vendor/ procurement relationship.

British Bobby is one of the best procurement professionals that I have ever dealt with. He epitomizes the characteristics listed above. Bobby was the VP of Procurement at this global conglomerate that I looked after. For a period of six months, I had connected with all of the executives in the company. I launched a massive campaign to get a deal done. The marketing was a success. The customer need was evident, and the relationships required to get a deal done were finally in place.

The last step was to get through procurement. When I first met with Bobby, he sat me down in his office. Bobby walked me through how he liked to work with vendors, what he was looking for in a sales rep, and how he wanted to negotiate this deal **(Integrity/Honesty)**. Bobby told me that he wanted to have an enduring relationship between our two companies. He wanted to make sure that his company got a good deal yet he didn't want us to bleed for doing it **(Long Term Perspective)**. He wanted to make sure that we had enough margin in the deal to be successful as well.

This was music to my ears. Any sales rep that hears this starts to smile on the inside. Perfect! This is exactly what we want as well! Unfortunately, I wasn't buying any of this; I'd been to this goat rodeo before way too many times, unfortunately. Clichés are clichés for a reason. So I'm going to use one right now: the proof is in the pudding. Put simply, I wanted to see him walk the talk.

Over the next four months of contract negotiations, Bobby was true to his word. Every time he pushed us to the brink on a legal or business issue, I stood my ground and told Bobby we were on the edge. At that point, Bobby backed off to make sure that we wouldn't bleed. Bobby was incredibly good at what he did. He extracted some amazing conditions for his company but he did it with integrity, transparency, and a long-term perspective.

Throughout the process, I got to know Bobby a lot better. He talked about his wife, his hobbies, and things he did that brought him joy.

When we got to the closing stage and he was ready to sign, I asked Bobby if we could do the official signing over dinner. It was a big deal for our company and I wanted to commemorate the moment. As the wine was flowing, we let our guards down even more. Bobby told me about his son who had died of cancer (**Authentic**). At that moment, we both shed tears and realized what was truly important.

Bobby was one of the best procurement professionals that I have ever worked with. What made us get along so famously was that we were mature enough to realize that we were two sides of the same coin. He was working hard to do what was best for his company, while I was simultaneously doing the same for mine. We had shared interests in making sure that both of us were successful in the long run because if any of the implementations went south, he would need my help to fix it. Also, if we were bleeding on the deal, then there would be no incentive or probably no mechanism for me to help him out.

When sales managers are hiring for sales reps or when companies look at their account executives, what characteristics or attributes do you think they are looking for? If sales and procurement are two sides of the same coin, wouldn't we be looking for the exact same attributes in a sales rep as we did in a procurement professional? What do you think? I'd love to hear from you.

Lessons Learned:

- Be authentic and your true self. Smart people will see through any façade you might inadvertently put up.

- Keep a long-term perspective on relationships. The more you invest in them now, the more they will pay back in the long run.

- Talent and skill will take you up to a certain level. Integrity and honesty will keep you there.

DISCLAIMER: *All of the events and situations in this story are based on true events. Peter ended up hiring Trong and giving him his first corporate sales job. Against her better judgment, Natalie gave Trong an opportunity to* *be a life-partner. Trong is still disappointed that the only playa in his house is the cassette playa he got in ninth grade.*

19.

UNPRECEDENTED, IMPOSSIBLE TO TOP

By Camille Clemons

I may have the platform, but the team deserves the credit.

In my industry, events happen throughout the year attended by participants in a specific sector, geographical location, strategy, or product. Depending on the event, a firm may send one or more of their team members to "cover" the event: this involves talking to attendees, working a booth, holding meetings, etc. In this specific case, there were two representatives from my firm, about 2,500 attendees at the conference, and we did not have a booth, so all meetings were either prearranged or impromptu. In other words, no one was coming to us. The story to follow is not typical, but I hope you have an event as monumental in your career as this one was for mine.

On day one of a three-day conference in New York, I was finishing up a meeting when my other attending colleague called and asked if I could help. "Meet me in five minutes," they said. With a conference this size, it is not uncommon to run into many people you know, but at this time in our industry, firms were specialized and it was not common to see someone from a different sector or product line attending a specialized conference like this one - or so I thought.

I said "sure", because being a team player is one of the single most powerful tools you can have. We walked to a quieter part of the conference where 1:1 meetings could be held and you could meet the prospect. It just so happened, in this scenario, that I was the product expert. I'd taken some time out of the sales field to build out a product for our firm and it was the focus of this particular conference. Our prospect was a long-time friend (and former client) of my colleague who had received a blind bid from us on a new product he was working to bring to market. While we had never met, the credibility I had by association with my colleague was evident. Through our discussion and insightful line of questions, I was able to build additional credibility for our firm that put us in a position where we knew *exactly* what we needed to do to win the deal.

We asked him to give us 24 hours to determine whether or not we could get where we needed to be. They were launching a new product and the start-up costs associated were making their choice to work with us difficult, as the up-front expenses were material. Nonetheless, they knew that we were the right choice...in the long-term anyway. We shook hands, walked away, and then spent the following hours tracking down the appropriate partners (several of whom were attending the conference) involved in the deal. This was going to require some creativity, flexibility, and resourcefulness.

We rolled up our sleeves and got to work. I called Don from Cleveland – his front-end costs were higher than the competition but we found a way of wrapping them into ongoing costs so as to spread them over a longer period of time. The same was true for four of the five firms involved – each one we called was willing to hear the story and figure out a way to make it happen. My last call was to Mark in Tulsa. Mark was known for being inflexible – especially when it came to pricing. I explained the opportunity here to Mark – we had a chance to be part of something special. He ultimately was the lynchpin in our ability to win or lose this deal. It took some work, but he came through in the end.

Before I give away the ending, it is important to point out a couple of things:

- This prospect had a strong history of success.

- Everyone is your client, including your vendors and internal team members. The stronger your relationships, the easier it is to find collaborative and creative solutions.

- Building relationships by having a genuine desire to get to know people is key to your success - you can't fake this part.

- Use your gut to know who you can take chances on; you don't have an unlimited number of requests like this.

- Hard work and creative thinking pay off.

By the next morning at 11 am, we had confirmed with all of the necessary people and were prepared to present our updated proposal. We came through on all of the requests and when we were able to meet the prospect at 2 pm that afternoon, less than 24 hours since our initial meeting, we had closed the deal, shook hands and finished out the conference with a little more swagger than when we started.

In addition to the bullet points above, one of the other big takeaways is to be open and careful about having too narrow a scope when talking to anyone in business. This former client was attending a conference that was adjacent to the business where we knew them, and they were looking to launch a different type of product. Successful people find many paths to success, so keep a tight-knit network and be sure to keep in touch; you never know when you may be needed.

20.

WHAT ARE YOU SCARED OF?

By Trong Nguyen

It's fascinating that as a kid everything seems so much bigger than it really is. Your dad seems to be this Goliath that could squash the Hulk with his pinky. The snow banks around the neighborhood look like they could dwarf Mt. Everest, or at least Mt. Rainer.

As adults, little really changes. We usually make a bigger deal out of things than they really are. Our highs are really high and our lows are really low. In the corporate world, we especially apply this optic when it comes to hierarchy.

Heuristics is the study of human decision-making that was first developed by Israeli psychologists Amos Tversky and Daniel Kahneman. Simply put, it is how we use experience and practical shortcuts to solve complex problems. This helps us to acquire immediate answers during long cognitive processing when the best solution is impossible or impractical.

In sales, we consciously use this methodology every day to influence our customers. Whether it is the anchoring, familiarity, or escalation of commitment heuristic, we use it to our advantage to further the sales process.

However, what happens when we don't recognize that we are unconsciously applying a heuristic to our professional or personal life? How much of a disadvantage are we at? I would argue to you that it is quite a bit.

Sometimes we inadvertently use positional authority or hierarchy as a heuristic on ourselves. When we meet the CXO or President of a company, we immediately think that they must be special or that they are graced with some magical talent that we are not blessed with.

I was like Russell Crowe in *Gladiator*: completely unstoppable. If you wanted to close the game-changing deals, if you wanted to blow out the numbers, if you wanted to overthrow empires, you called me. I was the closer.

And then I went home. I would run the house like I ran my business at work. I was shouting out orders quicker than Rain Man could count numbers or matchsticks. God, it felt good; I had arrived. But then reality hit. In under a minute, my wife and three kids put me in my place.

They didn't care what I did at work, what kind of multi-million dollar deals I had just closed or how much money we just made. All they knew was that I was their dad and I was there to help them with homework, change their diapers, and cook my sinfully delicious pancakes on-demand.

It would be years later until I began to appreciate what I really had at home. I had a mechanism that grounded me and brought me back to earth. No matter how big my head or ego got, I was reminded when I got home that I was as normal as everyone else.

Bill Gates was once asked in an interview, "You are the richest and most powerful man in the world. What's your life like at home? Do your kids obey your every command?" Bill said, "Kids are kids. My kids don't know who Bill Gates is, they just know that I am their dad."

I get asked a lot by new sales reps, "Trong, how do you spend time with all of these senior executives and how do you build such symbiotic relationships? How do I get to that level of excellence?" The answer usually surprises them.

I tell them the senior execs that we work with are just normal people; they have the same problems that we all have. This answer usually surprises them. The new sales reps think that there is just some magic or voodoo I must be conjuring up in order to get the results that I get.

To prove my point, I invite senior executives from our customers into our account planning sessions. When they are there, I do a one-hour Q&A session with these executives. I probe with a lot of personal questions. Where were they born? Where did they live? I ask about their families, where they went to school, etc.

By the time we are done, my team is usually floored. I've just taken one of the top executives that we work with as our customers and made them human. They have the same home issues that we have. They help with homework, change diapers, and are secretly scared of their wives as well!

Here's an example of the questions I ask on a cue card.

Jane Smith - Global CIO Questions

1. Where were you born? How many brothers and sisters do you have?

2. Where did you go to school?

3. Did you consider careers other than banking?

4. What do you like to do in your spare time? What do you like to do for fun?

5. What's your greatest strength? What do you need to improve on?

6. If you could change one thing about you, what would it be?

7. Name a vendor or partner that you think really highly of. Why?

8. What's the most difficult part of the job? What's the most fun part of the job?

9. You've spent a lot of time in different parts of the business, how has this helped you prepare for your current role?

10. Who are some leaders you look to? Why?

11. Looking back on your career, would you have done anything differently?

12. If money were not an issue and you could do anything you want as a profession, what would you do?

The next time you are out with a senior executive and are nervous because of their title and/or position, just remember that they are like everyone else. Ultimately, we are all just people. When you come from that perspective, everything else will fall into place.

Lessons Learned:

- CXOs and top executives are just normal people; don't be scared of them. They have the same issues and problems as the rest of us. They put on their pants one leg at a time, just like the rest of us.

- Inviting top executives to meet and talk to your team will humanize them and provide you with a different perspective. It gives the executive a chance to meet and understand the motivations behind your team. It gives your team a chance to understand what makes the executive "tick."

- Beware of biases and heuristics such as positional authority, as they will inevitably change how you should behave. Read works from the godfathers of human psychology and decision-making – Amos Tversky and Daniel Kahneman.

- Find creative and fun ways to integrate customer executives into your planning and business development sessions. They will provide more insight than if you just had an internal meeting.

- Let your team help shape the agenda and the format of your account planning sessions. This ensures that they get what they need out of the session.

- Bring your executives and leadership team to the account planning session. They need to be an integral part of your business.

- When customers are part of the process, they feel more vested in making you successful as well. They now have a stake in the game, so to speak.

- Read Michael Lewis' new book *The Undoing Project: A Friendship That Changed Our Minds*. It is a great book that delves into the origins of heuristics and how Amos Tversky and Daniel Kahneman shaped how we think.

21.

SELL HIGH

By Jacquelyn Nicholson

Early in my career, I worked for a very big Fortune 50-100 company. At the time, I wasn't yet a quota-carrying salesperson, but was in a sales-like position. I was in a role leading a massive global project for an internal center of excellence at the shared service organization within the company that essentially had me selling the services that we managed for them. So in fact, I was selling, albeit internally, and it was actually the reason I got into sales. It was a great experience and was something that shaped my career and sparked my desire to go into sales full-time externally.

In order to get this global project approved, budget secured, and the infrastructure initiative started, I was tasked with going around to the entire staff of our CIO to sell them on this massive effort we were about to undertake; a great opportunity for someone who was in their 20s.

Never mind the fact that I wasn't working for a manager, which was traditional. I was reporting to a director, which was unusual in the hierarchy of this company. My director was then called onto a special project and after the project approval I ended up reporting directly to the Vice President of our division for the next several months.

My director and my VP invested a lot of trust and faith in me and asked me to lead the presentation and to sell the idea and specifics of the project to the CIO and his staff. My director spent a ton of time coaching me and told me what to do. To this very day, I'm forever grateful to him for all he taught me. I was to go around and interview everyone on the CIO's direct staff in advance of the meeting in order to make sure that, prior to the day of the CIO's staff meeting, we had a buy-in from everybody.

I spent several weeks scheduling meetings with very senior executives of the company who reported to the CIO. When I briefed my director about all of my findings, I was so proud. He also was thrilled. It was funny, though, as I ticked off all the people I had met: Danny, Tom, Kevin and Jeff... it was at that point during the conversation that my boss reacted in complete and utter disbelief! He said, "Why the hell did you meet with that guy!?!?" I said, "Well, you told me to meet everybody on the CIO's staff!" He said, "He doesn't work for the CIO, he works for the Vice Chairman of the Board!" I am pretty sure at this point that I turned several increasingly paler shades of white. I was thinking that I was in big trouble, but actually, he started laughing and said, "Well, what did he say?!" I responded that I met with him for over 90 minutes and that he was very excited to hear that.

He shook his head and I assume he had a flashback to an interview question he had asked me a year ago. He told me to describe a situation that intimidated me and what I would do about it. I sat there for a moment and was dumbfounded, giving it some thought and then some more. After careful consideration, I told him the following, "I'm really sorry but honestly I can't think of anything. I don't mean to be difficult, but if I do think of anything, I will call you back."

Several months after the project was successfully completed, that extra person I interviewed summoned me to a meeting. You know... the one who did not report to the CIO, but to the Vice Chairman. It was a pretty large group of people and I noticed amongst the suits that I was the only woman, definitely the youngest, and, for certain, the most junior. I knew many of them, all senior management, directors, and those above. As the Vice Chair's direct report greeted everyone, it was a very serious handshake and deep-toned "Very nice to meet you." When he saw me, he shouted, "Jacquelyn! How are you? How is Murphy?" It was priceless to see. His face broke out in a huge grin; he happily shook my hand with his other hand, also enclosing mine in a friendly kind handshake, and completely dumbfounded the entire group of people. It meant the world to me. I had taken the time to meet him several months ago in my fearless ignorance of his senior title but managed to form a relationship after that without intimidation. Those efforts gave me the right to have access to his insights and to be invited to meetings I would otherwise have not been able to join. It also enabled me to see senior executives as people just like you and me, who want to be liked for who they are, and who are mostly regular folks just looking to be valued and for people to listen. That experience taught me to approach the C suite in my career often and easily, enabling me to meet a variety of CEOs, CMOs, CIOs, VPs and Board of Director members over the decades since. I treasure it.

22.

ASK FOR REFERRALS
OFTEN AND ALWAYS

By Kevin Walkup

Trust that doing good business means that good things will come of it. At a very young age, I learned that referrals are one of the best ways to do business. Growing up, my mom ran a catering business. Our phone was constantly ringing with people asking her to do luncheons, wedding showers, and even funerals. She couldn't make enough food to keep up with the pace of all the people wanting her business. As a young kid, I didn't think much of it. I just thought "that's how business is done. People just naturally want to buy from you." If it were only that easy! In college, I took a marketing class where I quickly discovered that marketing was not my forte, although parts of it certainly peaked my interest. I asked my mom what kind of marketing she did for her business. "Marketing?" she asked. "I give out my business card at every event and tell my customers to feel free to share with their friends." Zero marketing. Zero websites. Zero Google paid ads. Her business was 100% organic and referral based. She never made anyone feel like they were being sold to, as such. Her customers wanted her to cater their events because their friends and colleagues raved about how delicious her food was.

I was lucky to have learned to do business in this way. Make it a win/win scenario for everyone. Build your own brand of having done great business. If you do it right, people will talk about it, they will self-promote it; at the end of the day, you end up getting to choose which business to accept from others, rather than chasing new sales. This all stems from a mentality, a certain being that one possesses about caring and respecting those that one does business with, as well as earning their long-term trust. Long-term trust is equal to long-term business with organic referrals.

Trust yourself that you do good business. Trust and be confident that the solution you are providing will help your customers, as well as people they know. If you've built a trusting relationship with your buyers, they will happily refer you to others. It makes that ask so much easier:

"Hi [New Customer], I've really enjoyed earning your business over the last few months and I am constantly striving to improve and earn more business. Who else in your network may get the same value out of the solution that I have provided for you? Would you be willing to make a warm introduction?"

Asking for referrals shouldn't feel foreign. Happy customers are willing to give them and the best salespeople don't mind asking for them. You can ask often and always, even to a prospect you've disqualified. If you're a pro at building rapport early on in a deal cycle, you can ask for referrals as early as the first conversation. However, make sure to have provided value before asking.

Providing a great buying experience is just the beginning. When you're genuine, authentic, and empathetic in your sales approach, you build trust with your buyers. Once you've earned that trust, it opens the doors for more opportunities... more SALES opportunities.

Just like in my next story, you never want to burn a bridge. Your network and relationships can easily become a source for generating new business. Organic referrals are great. Ask for referrals. Maintaining long-term relationships is worth more than you think.

Doing good business will ultimately bring about organic referrals. However, why not be proactive with your network and generate new opportunities by easily asking who else may value your time? If done right, you remove the feeling of being the "salesperson" and become the "business consultant" to create a concrete foundation to help someone else's business. Your customers will appreciate it.

Referrals don't have to be just asking for other prospects' business. Referrals can help you move your sale to the next opportunity stage by getting you intel on who you're talking to, what's important to them, or how to say something that will get them even more engaged. It's leveraging your network down the road when you see they're connected with someone that you've previously done good business with. Referrals can happen months or even years later. They can open a door that may have seemed closed. People will talk to people they know and will make time for people they're recommended to speak with.

These aren't just free deals you're going to win without doing any work; they are a way into a conversation that you may not have had the ability to have before.

Case in point: I had my house painted recently. The painter did a great job. I wrote him his check, we shook hands, and he began to walk away. He stopped, turned around, and said, "Mr. Kevin, please, if you know any of your friends that would like painting work done, please give them my information." This made me so happy. Not only was I happy about the work he had done for me, but I was happy to suggest his work to others. After all of these years of asking for referrals, I was now the buyer and getting a taste of my own medicine. I loved it. Just like the people I have sold to in the past that have given referrals, I was happy to help. When he asked the question, I immediately started thinking of people that I could reach out to that were in a similar situation to me.

If I came up short with immediate referrals, I knew that whenever that conversation came up, he would be my best point of contact. Your network is your bloodline. I received his information from a contact that I trust, a referral. My contact is making my life easier, the painter is making my life easier and my painter's life is made easier because he knows if he does good work, his network will work for him as long as he asks for those referrals.

23.

MAKE A HABIT OF BITING YOUR TONGUE, SO THE CLIENT HAS TIME TO SPEAK

By Trey Simonton

In July of 2012, I had just started as a new Account Executive at a large social media company with an enterprise software platform focused on ratings and reviews. At the time, the company well-established with a solid reputation for empowering the voice of the consumer with many of the world's largest online retailers. A trend was underway, with banks and insurance companies who were trying to improve their online reputation; the company already had many of the largest financial institutions as customers.

I saw the focus on financial services as a tremendous opportunity for me personally. The reason for this, was because I had a fair amount of experience selling into these institutions, understood how to demonstrate value and had experience addressing their concerns tied to security and personal information. I voiced my desire and passion for focussing in this area and soon had a number of large financial services accounts assigned to my territory.

Six weeks into my tenure, a meeting was secured in Boston with a large property and casualty insurer. I was excited because ten client contacts with roles ranging from Director to AVP and Vice President had confirmed they would be attending the meeting. The Boston company was suffering from a declining online reputation, and senior executives at the firm were curious how ratings and reviews might help them "tell a better story" about why their clients love their products and services.

As I was aware of the scheduled attendees, I invited my DVP and a Senior Client Success manager to attend and help support me in the meeting. The client gave us just over an hour for the presentation, and we killed it. We spent almost fifty minutes highlighting the benefits of our platform, how we protected financial institutions and showed we could absolutely help them with their declining online reputation. We left ten minutes for the client to answer questions and review next steps. The client had a number of questions and continued talking, sharing their feedback, for another fifteen minutes after the meeting concluded. *Great meeting right...* I looked forward to debriefing with my DVP.

Afterward, we walked to a nearby coffee shop to sit as a team and discuss the presentation and review next steps. My DVP was quick to compliment us, "You guys clearly know financial services, and your understanding of the Bazaarvoice platform is impressive, BUT you completely missed the client's questions early in the meeting about how our solution would help them." This comment caught me off guard, but as I thought about it, we talked A LOT! The DVP continued, "Moving forward, I would like you to begin biting your tongue as much as you can when you are tempted to speak, making sure you are giving time for the client to speak. The group had a lot to say, and you guys weren't listening. In fact, in a 30-minute meeting, try to bite your tongue six times. In a 60 minute meeting, try to bite your tongue eleven times!"

The concept of biting my tongue resonated with me. It would force me to take a moment to listen even when I had something "brilliant" to share. I looked for ways to reinforce this habit and began placing small tick marks in my moleskin where I took notes; this ensured I was biting my tongue six to eleven times based on the duration of the meeting.

In a 30 minute meeting try to bite your tongue SIX times

In a 60 minute meeting try to bite your tongue ELEVEN times

To this day, you can pick up my moleskin and see multiple tick marks in the top corners of the pages. If you see six or more tick marks, you can rest assured I had a pretty successful 30-minute meeting. If you see eleven or more tick marks, well you know this was a successful hour-long meeting, to say the least...

24.

YOUR NETWORK IS EVERYTHING

By Kevin Walkup

Asmart business person will never burn a bridge. Leaving my last company was one of the hardest decisions I've ever made. Having landed some of the best accounts in the world (companies in which I am still invested, which is another story altogether), I had no reason to look elsewhere. My boss and I shared a special bond; he knew he could count on me to produce and build relationships with the right people within the right accounts. He taught me to write down my goals, to keep them top of mind, and to strive towards exceeding them every day. Physically, checking off a goal as complete is incredibly rewarding and I highly recommend experiencing that type of satisfaction. At the time, I was 25 years old and I was incredibly driven by money; in fact, I still am. I once told my boss that one of my goals was to make $100,000 in one year. That sounded like more money than I could ever spend. It felt like he took this as a personal challenge and he held me to it. He made sure that I didn't lose sight and had me draft a plan for how I would accomplish my goal. I will never forget the day that he walked up to my desk, handed me a box, and said "congratulations." In the box was a watch. He had been tracking my progress and knew I had hit my goal. This was over 6 years ago and I am wearing the watch still as I write this. I think about him every day when I put it on; he was like a father figure to me. When it was time for me to leave that company to pursue a career in software sales, it was a tough conversation. I could have quit like the guy in the movie "Half Baked." One's personal network is too important to do that. I know better than to burn a bridge. Steve understood my decision and told me that the lights will always be on if I ever wanted to come back.

Fast forward 4 years and I am introduced to an SVP at a multi-billion dollar organization, where we have a great conversation. He tells me he is the ultimate decision-maker; however, I need to win over his counterpart, John, in order to proceed. The SVP makes an intro and John replies almost immediately:

"Please send me an invitation for 12 noon central time next Wednesday. I have 30 minutes. Show me/tell me/Wow me."

"John gets straight to the point and doesn't mess around," I thought. This guy is not going to be easy. I need to do some homework on John, so I look him up on LinkedIn. Much to my surprise, I see John is connected to my old boss. Steve is in a completely different industry, so it's not like they're just randomly connected. I then shoot a quick text to Steve asking about how he knows John. Seconds later, my phone rings. It's Steve. He couldn't believe I just dropped the name of one of his best friends. I tell him about the situation and about the half-ass email I just received from John. He laughs and isn't surprised. He tells me he will call him. The following Monday morning, I receive this email from John:

"Okay, you just earned an hour :-)"

Steve Hurst called me Friday night. "I understand he hired you as a young sales rep in Atlanta. I have almost a 25-year history with that man. Not only is he one of my closest friends on this planet, but he was my business partner. Together as very young guys, we built a world-class business in Columbus Ohio. My SVP, Barry, met him at my wedding. He tells me that you're a younger version of me. That was absolutely quite something to hear. He told me the story about the watch he gave you and what you're made of. I'm looking forward to meeting with you and hearing what you have and how it might help us."

The relationship I kept with Steve over the years changed the entire shape and speed of my conversation with John. I was now walking into a warm room as a trusted advisor carrying some clout, rather than meeting with someone that was taking a call because his boss told him to do so. 2 years later, John and I continue to stay in touch and he has become a mentor to me.

Had I departed from my last company like Scarface did from Half Baked, my relationship with Steve would have been tarnished and I therefore wouldn't have been walked into an incredible opportunity with an incredible organization. Another mentor of mine, Ralph Barsi, once told me, "if you treat people as if they have a ten on their head, good things will come of it. It may not be today, tomorrow or even next month, but you will be remembered and it will pay off." Your personal brand works for you 24/7. What is gone today may come back tomorrow in a different shape or form. Allow your network to walk you into accounts with a warm handshake and a smile. Your personal brand and network will help accelerate your sales process, win more deals, and earn more referrals.

25.

WHY LUNCH DOESN'T MATTER

By Trong Nguyen

I want to tell you a story. Like all good stories, you have to read between the lines to see what's really going on. However, the verses and the refrain of this particular story can be universally applied to all of us. It's not just my story; it's everybody's. I had been asked to join Microsoft as a sale rep to tackle one of their toughest customers. This customer was highly decentralized and scattered throughout the USA. They had their own unique culture and Microsoft had burned through account managers every year with the hope that someone would be able to find the secret to cracking this customer. On the surface, this customer seemed irrational, overly demanding, and completely wrapped up in their own little bubble. They didn't like the way we did things. Didn't they know who we were? We are Microsoft! Everyone wants to buy our stuff...

Right?

In a short period of time, I was able to turn around the relationships. It's all in the approach, as it turns out, and I had the right one. I soon became a trusted advisor with most of the C-Suite. As a result, the CFO, COO, CMO and senior executives always took my meetings. These relationships helped us to build the bridge that was necessary to make this customer a vanguard in their industry. They were one of the first customers in a highly-regulated industry to go to the cloud. For instance, Office

365 enabled them to become highly agile, effectively integrating their many disparate acquisitions and truly enabling employee collaboration.

Back at Microsoft, we were on cloud nine (no pun intended). We had cracked the code and were able to get one of our toughest customers to embrace us and the future – cloud computing. Like most great process and analytics companies, we started doing some forensics, deal reviews, and analysis to see how we could cookie cutter this alchemy onto other businesses and recreate this same win with them as well. Could I repeat the magic? That was the question.

When they went through my time and expense reports for the previous two-year period, they hit the jackpot. Ding Ding Ding! We have the answer! Our analysts found out that for the most part, every breakfast, lunch, and dinner I'd had over that two-year period were with customers. There was a complete correlation. You have meals with your customers in order to build relationships. These relationships help build trust. Once you build trust, then you can close massive deals to achieve your quota. Wash, rinse, repeat. The answer was so plain and simple, we wondered why we hadn't seen it before.

When the analysis was revealed, I chuckled a bit. It made me think about a statistics professor I had in university. At the beginning of every class, he said, "There are lies, damned lies, and then there are statistics!" This little saying always stuck with me. It rings as true today as it did 110 years ago when Mark Twain first said it. The missing insight from the company's analysis was, "Why did Trong have so many of his meals with his customers?" If they had asked that question, they would have found out the real reason, for it was simple. The customer and I were so busy that this was the only time when we could meet. The customer was busy working on key initiatives to help transform their company, and I was busy helping with various initiatives that would enable the customer to execute such a transformation. In other words, we had common and shared goals. Eventually, as with all busy people, we had to eat at some point. We used those mealtimes to catch up and stay in sync and ensure that our projects were aligned.

When most new sales reps are out meeting with customers, one of the first things they invariably say is, "We should grab lunch…" I cringe every time I hear it because it is so cliché and neither side means it. Plus, the customer automatically starts to mentally paint the picture of a typical sales rep who adds no value but can still buy them a free meal.

At a minimum, it takes two hours to have lunch with a customer. Yes, that long! It's a minimum of 30 minutes to prepare for it. You have to do your background research. At least 30 minutes for travel. And then at a minimum, it is 60 minutes for lunch itself. That's a quarter of your workday. And that is assuming you don't have a "Don Draper" Mad Men lunch. Everyone is really busy. In our 24/7 world, could our time be better used?

Breakfast is the most important meal of the day. But – and hear me out – I would argue that you can miss lunch. Why? You'll be further ahead. The foundation of any meaningful and long-term relationship is shared experiences and shared goals. If the sales rep took those two hours that would have been spent on lunch and, instead, focused deeply on adding value to the customer and helping to solve the problems that their customers are working on, then that would become the foundation for their relationship. Now there are shared and common goals that can act as a bridge to building the desired relationships. It's not about drinks or a fancy meal. It's not about having a steak and a glass of wine, no matter how enjoyable that might be. No, that wasn't the point of my lunches. The point was to add value for the customer in the only time we had free.

The next time you are out on a sales call and are coaching a new sales rep, watch for the cues. Do they automatically jump to drinks, lunch, or dinner in order to build rapport or a relationship? Or do they go back to first principles to see what the issues and problems are and see how their solutions can help solve these customer problems?

What do you think? Does lunch really matter?

Lessons Learned:

- Focus on adding value to your customers. That is the north star that will lead you to build great customer relationships and close deals.

- Relationships are built on shared and common goals, so find out what those goals are with your customers. Use those as the bridge to building long-term relationships.

- Some social activities can be used to jumpstart relationships but long-term meaningful relationships develop through adding value and building trust. The social activities will naturally develop as a result of building that trust.

- Let your customers decide where to eat and what social activities to do. As sales reps, we do this every day, so it is not a big deal to us. For most customers, it is a treat for them to have that occasional lunch or dinner out. So let them decide the venue.

- Be wary of metrics and data that big companies compile. Taken out of context, they never truly tell the whole story. Metrics and data (like my T&E reports) can always be twisted to tell the story you want to tell.

- The general perception is that most sales reps are only good for paying for lunch and drinks. Don't fall into that stereotype. Focus on the work and the value. You will be so busy with your customer that meals and drinks will naturally flow as you start to bond through shared and common goals.

- When you are going through RFP stages or blackout periods, be sure to obey the rules. You don't want to inadvertently put your clients at risk by taking them out to lunch or dinner when you were not supposed to.

- When you are out with your clients, don't be afraid to let your guard down a little. For example, perhaps tell them about your family and personal life. The more that they see you as a person, the easier it will be for you to connect on an emotional level.

- At some point, your clients will ask you to connect with them on social media channels such as Facebook or Instagram. My recommendation is to do it! They trust and like you enough to open up their world to you – accept it and reciprocate.

26.

AVOID THE SINGLE THREAD - NEVER FAIL ALONE

By Jacquelyn Nicholson

When trying to close one of the largest multi-year SaaS deals I had ever been involved in, I learned the lesson that it's equally important to involve the right people internally, as well as to not be single-threaded externally. Often in sales, we recognize the need to not be selling to one person in a large enterprise deal. After all, it's vital to make sure you are hearing from all stakeholders, that you understand pain across the organization, and that you have a wide array of supporters, advocates and ultimately- customers.

What isn't always so obvious is the need to rally your internal troops, ALL of them. Not just your solutions experts or sales engineers, not just your boss, not just your executives, not just your head of design, not just your head of product or engineering and not just your customer success or services team. Everyone!

Well, of course, everyone who makes sense. ;)

When I first started our sales cycle, I had brought my VP with me, and the initial meeting went really well. It was clear to me, however, that this deal was large and would require my champion to be exposed to different parts of our organization beyond me and my boss, and if he was truly to be an advocate for us moving forward, he would need to have access across the organization.

Part one was ensuring we were the solution of choice. In my discussions, I came to realize that my buyer liked details and wanted to feel like he was on the inside of how we were building the company, as well as to understand what we were doing and why we were doing it. Enter our head of design and head of product - a fantastic duo of two of the smartest people I have had the honor of working with in my career. With these two, I didn't even need an agenda, nor did I need to talk much. My buyer brought his right-hand person along, and the four of them discussed a multitude of things, including design and aesthetics, as well as the direction the engineering team was taking with the product. It was perfect; I was fairly certain that my competitors weren't able to say the same, but I wasn't content yet at this point.

The next step was to involve our senior team. During our annual flagship customer conference, it made sense to invite my buyer to the senior executive dinner with our Customer Advisory Board. Normally, we reserve a few spots for our potential buyers to mingle with customers and executives, but for this guy, it really had to be genuine and authentic, not schmooze-y or fake. Because my company was one with a genuinely positive and authentic culture, this was pretty straightforward. By combining some great conversations with customers along with some serious luck, we hit a huge home run. Two senior people at the company also shared my buyer's favorite hobby; I had basically unleashed a wonderful tsunami of good vibes, literally.

After that, it came time to bring it home with the kind of support and relationship the buyer and his company would be receiving. We met with the head of customer success and basically walked through the tool at the highest level, talking about what was possible, what made sense for the buyer's team, and how we would support them. Again, it was all down to the emotion of the whole process, and we were hitting all the right marks.

Now it was time to wait. As the team did their evaluation, I sent over a thank you book on my potential customer's favorite hobby, personally signed by my President, which included a hand-written note from both of us. In a couple of weeks, I was rewarded three-fold: first with the business of this company for over three years, second with a relationship I still have to this day and third, with one of the best "You won the business" emails I have ever gotten. The new customer took the time to highlight how much we cared about their business, their business pain, and most of all, how many people from my company were invested in bringing the solution to light.

I will never forget it.

27.

SUCCESS FROM RELATIONSHIPS AND TRUST

By Paul DiVincenzo

I was driving down the 10 freeway in Los Angeles and received a call that one of my mentors and current Operation's Vice President was no longer going to be in his position... I pulled over and mentally wrestled with this for almost a half an hour. This working partner of mine had been a key component to my success over the last three years since my promotion into the Government vertical. He had been open-minded in tackling some of the hardest accounts in the government space within our region, and we had built that into a multi-million-dollar business. Most importantly, I had built an amazing working relationship with him and had the credibility to get things done within one conversation vs multiple meetings, so much so that many other people were jealous of me in my region and would (reluctantly) seek my counsel on how to approach him on deals. I wasn't sure who was going to be taking his position, but I knew that my approach and a key to my success had just been thrown a massive curveball. Furthermore, I needed to figure out how to navigate through and re-establish a foundation in order to continue to grow my current sales and future growth.

As with many new leaders, our new VP had a completely different way of operating and different structure he wanted to implement. This was very challenging in the beginning, as it was different than the way we had approached the business before; I felt as though he was intentionally trying to sabotage my sales. However, this wasn't the case; he simply had a mission and goal he needed to accomplish. There are many ways to look at these types of challenges; usually, most people take it personally, which will mostly impact performance in a way that is negative to themselves, their personal brand, and the company as a whole. One of the first things I have realized is that if you are an expert in your market, you have more credibility than you know. The first step is to become the expert and really understand what's going on in the market, as well as how you can explain that confidently to the leadership in a way that helps them realize that you can be an asset to them and help them achieve their goals. One of the biggest components that I found during this transition was that my new VP's goals initially did not seem to align with mine; he wanted to standardize products in a way that would not allow us to win in the marketplace. This meant removing about 30% of our product line from the marketplace that we had been selling in prior years, which had been a key to us winning some of the largest and most complex accounts in our region. He had looked at these as individual silos' and the profit margin on these was not great. In this evaluation process of silo thinking, we lost a 1.8 million dollar deal.

I had to remove myself from the situation mentally and re-evaluate my approach to our business, as well as how to teach the leadership about what it takes to win in the marketplace that we were in. One of the biggest challenges is to understand how other people think and how to better align with that so that we all "understand" each other to the point of gaining ***true trust***. Typically, this understanding of how people think and approach problems can help us find common ground and work together more efficiently. In this particular case, the VP needed to increase profit and, therefore, wanted to streamline the product line arbitrarily, as reducing the product line would increase the profit margin on the overall account in theory. However, if we didn't offer this 30% of the product line, we would simply not win any accounts, meaning we would lose 100% of the revenue.

I prepared a market analysis for two weeks, which I had learned how to do by building my government marketplace. I evaluated 10 large

industries and broke down each area and where we were using this product line we had been discussing. We found out that out of all the accounts
sold, this 30% product line only represented about 5% of revenue. In
other words, our risk in this investment was limited to a very small percentage of the overall revenue. As we discussed these accounts, he realized that provided we standardize this additional 30% and put some rules
around it, we could win more deals and reduce costs across the region
without losing any ground to the competition. Through this presentation, additional conversations and 2 to 3 meetings internally, we created
a new market strategy *together* that allowed us to continue to win deals
in our competitive market space. We would offer non-standard products,
but standardize those across our region. Most importantly, I built an
amazing relationship with the new VP with trust and credibility so that
I could continue to win in the marketplace with executive support. Over
3 years later, my relationship with this new VP is as strong as that of my
old VP, if not stronger, and we continue to work on large complex deals
together in a collaborative manner to find solutions, as opposed to simply
having rules dictated down, which isn't fun and rarely helps anyone.

Lessons Learned:

1. When a challenge is thrown your way, take some time to
   evaluate it.

2. Try to understand how to align the goals of leadership
   with your own.

3. Become a trusted advisor to leadership and "partner up"
   with them on the approach.

4. Build trust and alignment with the highest level of leadership
   and they will endorse you to help your brand internally.

Sales Careers

28.

CHOOSING A NEW PATH IN SALES

By John Hinkson

For more than 20 years I worked in manufacturing, and it was usually in a supervisory or management role. Over time, I became dissatisfied with the daily grind. The daily processes of dealing with personnel issues and operations became very mundane to me. Even though I met and exceeded our production goals every month, I felt there were no new challenges, and as a consequence, I lost all enthusiasm for my work.

As this feeling of dissatisfaction and regret continued to grow because of my chosen career path, I started looking for something that would make me feel better. I decided I would go and buy a new car! I always loved purchasing a new car. Everything about it from the new car smell, to the general sense of excitement of actually getting a new car, has always made me happy. This time it was different; the excited feeling didn't last long because I couldn't shake the nagging feeling of dissatisfaction. I had purchased the car at my hometown dealership, as always, and found myself thinking about my actual experience of buying that new car.

I enjoyed the atmosphere of the dealership, the friendly feeling, the smiles on everyone's faces and I kept thinking about how good I had felt while I was at the dealership for the purchase. I continued to think about my experience, and after 3 months I decided to go back and ask for a job.

I didn't tell anyone that I was planning to do this simply because I wasn't sure the dealership would consider hiring me. I had no sales experience, and my personality was not what most people believed to be the typical "car salesman."

However, I achieved an interview, and while I was very excited to get this opportunity, I still wasn't sure I would get the job. During the interview with the General Manager, I remember talking about how I really would love to have this opportunity and felt I could be successful even though I had no experience selling cars. We talked about my experience in manufacturing and my role as a manager. It was then he pointed out to me that to lead the people working for me I was selling myself every day.

I got the job! I went home feeling so excited about this new challenge, all the possibilities in this new career and feeling very hopeful about the future. When I shared this great news with my family, I was very surprised to find out that my wife did not share my enthusiasm. She was furious. She said I had lost my mind, that I was having a midlife crisis. I reached out to my mother for some support and ran into the same arguments. She said I would starve to death, that it was better to have a guaranteed paycheck, and that a car salesperson starves during the winter.

With no support from my family, I began to doubt myself. For a few minutes, I questioned the decision I had made to go into car sales. I started to wonder if it was better to have a guaranteed paycheck even if I was unhappy with the work. But I knew that this was the career for me, I was excited about the possibilities, and I knew I would succeed.

I was nervous and scared when I started off on this new adventure, and I discovered what I had known all along. That this was the career for me and I had been right to believe so strongly in myself! The first month I sold 36 units! Not only did I sell a lot of cars, but I was enjoying meeting new people, and I really felt that I was helping people. I realized very quickly that not only could I make more money, but I could change the way people view car sales. I could be straightforward and honest and help more people than I ever had in my previous career. I continued to increase the number of my sales from, 42 units, 45 units, 50 units and more. Selling more cars and making the car buying experience something positive for everyone I met.

After being in car sales for 2 years, I wanted to learn more about Finance, so I spent 4 months in the Finance department. While it was an excellent learning experience, I missed sales too much, so I decided to return to it. After 3 years and 8 months, I have $45,340,318 in car sales with 1,948 units sold. I have enjoyed every step of this journey, and I know I have truly found my calling.

I was raised with the idea that you go to work, you do your job, and you get paid. Nowhere along the way did anyone say I should be happy in what I was doing, and I should try to find what excites me. I am very thankful I did not listen to the negative people. I believed in myself and was able to break out the daily grind of just collecting a paycheck.

- Listen to the inner voice telling you it's time for a change.

- Don't be afraid to go for what peaks your interest and excites you.

- Don't choose what's easy when you feel led to something else in your life.

29.

JUST F@#$ING KILL ME

By David Weiss

There I was, 22 years old, sitting in my college fraternity house, having just quit my first job out of school after only four months. This job was paying me more money than I thought possible, doing something I wanted to do for the rest of my life. I was scared. I felt like I had just made a crazy mistake and I did not understand what to do next.

Before I go further and discuss how I moved on to my next job—and ultimately an amazing career in sales—let me take you back four months.

I was working for a very large robotics company, selling solutions to automate factories. My territory was the state of New York. I lived in Rochester, New York; however, the regional office of the company I worked for was in Ramsey, New Jersey—roughly 400 miles away. The company I worked for had a rule that seemed to make sense at the time; their sales reps needed to be in the office Mondays and Fridays to set up meetings for the following week. This meant I was commuting 400 miles to work on Sunday, 400 miles home Monday night, running a territory the size of New York State Tuesday – Thursday, and then commuting back Thursday night to the office and 400 miles home again on Friday. While I could have stayed in New Jersey over the weekend to minimize my travel, I also wanted to have a life, and my life was back in Rochester.

This was during the winter. If you have never lived in that part of the country during the winter, I'll tell you this—snow, ice, and overall weather conditions are not conducive for this amount of travel. However,

I was doing it weekly. Sometimes I would drive, sometimes I would fly. The easiest airport for me to fly into was John F Kennedy, more fondly known as JFK, which stood for, Just F@#$ing Kill Me. I slept in that airport more times than I could count. By the way, I hate flying.

Now if all this wasn't enough to burn anyone out, this company also had no sales training. I knew nothing about time and territory management. So, I was all over the place. If anyone spoke to me, I would meet them in person, whenever they wanted, wherever they were. This made for some long days and nights. Suffice it to say, I made a huge career mistake and didn't have the foundational knowledge to solve for this obstacle. Good or bad, me as a person, I have almost no patience. So I looked this situation squarely in the eye and said, "I'm done."

Now, full circle, I'm sitting in my fraternity house, 22 years old, no job, money running out, asking myself, "What should I do next...?"

Thank God for Google. I had committed to sales as a career path. I loved it—the freedom, the money, the power to influence and ability to impact a business like no other position. I was hooked, but I was an untrained neophyte, and I knew I needed to fix that. So, I Googled "Companies with the best sales training." Fortunately, a publication called "Selling Power" came up. It was a GOLDMINE. It listed the companies with the best sales training and which also paid the best. So, what would any entrepreneurial sales person do? I applied to all of them... all 50 companies.

Aramark called me back. I spent four years there. They have some of the best sales training in the world. One of the first things they taught me was time and territory management—how to grid out a territory to be in certain areas on certain days and when to say, "No," to travel. Man, had I only known that a few months prior! But I won't digress.

I learned in a short time about how much I DIDN'T know about sales. They taught me various methodologies, styles, appreciative inquiry, closing skills, how to prospect, how to manage a pipeline, etc. They gave me a solid foundation from which I could grow. Now, I have learned a lot since then, and I will write about some things in another story, but the decision to join a company with solid sales training set me on the path to sales success.

As I look back on this chapter of my life, I'm happy I dared to recognize I was going down a path that would limit my long-term growth. What may seem like an obvious choice now, was a very difficult one then. I try to live by the philosophy of failing fast, learning from it and not making the same mistake again. This may mean I take more risks than others, but it has also put me on a faster path to success. The desire to not repeat past mistakes led me to find a company with good training and to realize the importance of building a strong foundation from a company that knows what they are doing with sales.

30.

LOVE THE PRODUCT YOU SELL

By George Penyak

This was a lesson I learned the hard way. It was at a print advertising company where I took on one of my first sales roles. It was around 2010 (and we all remember the economic climate back then) and the local newspaper had an opening for an advertising rep. A friend of mine worked there, who mentioned the position to me and recommended that I submit my resume. So I did, without studying the segment, learning the company's position in the marketplace, or doing much research at all. I thought to myself, *"Hey, some people still read the newspaper, right?"*

The question I should've asked myself is, "Do I still read the paper?" or "What do I already know about the paper or what is being advertised in it?" However, I didn't ask those questions. I did not challenge myself on why I was taking on a sales job to represent a product that I do not really see a future for; I just jumped right in.

This was detrimental to my success at the company.

After wrapping up training, I started making calls and setting appointments to meet with potential customers, mostly local businesses wanting to place ads in the newspaper.

I then began cold-calling local businesses, performing the everyday activities to meet as many potential customers as I could, making proposals and doing presentations.

However, something about the role never felt genuine to me; I never felt fully comfortable asking for an investment from a small business owner to advertise in the paper I represented. I felt there were so many other ways an owner could better spend their hard-earned money in the advertising space other than a printed ad.

Half-way through my short tenure at the company, this was my conclusion. I did not believe that print advertising in the newspaper was an effective way to market a small business and there was no way to convince me otherwise. Bear in mind that this is my opinion, and whether that is the case or not, this was (is) my belief, which showed through in my interactions, presentations, and proposals.

My close rate, my commissions, and my motivation to keep pushing forward were all low.

I lasted less than a year in that role and my short tenure ended after the newspaper and I mutually agreed to go our separate ways.

I look back today and I feel like it seeped out of me when I met new prospects and did the day to day grind. Long story short, this greatly affected my success at the company. I didn't realize this at the time, but after moving on to a company that better suited me (and had a service I could truly back), the difference was more than noticeable.

It is so hard for one to give their best effort to a product or service that they do not believe in themselves. I feel you will really stop being you, and if you're naturally gifted with a skillset that lends itself well to sales, that skillset will never fully show itself.

Have you ever listened to someone who spoke and said to yourself, "That person is passionate!"? Most of the time, they come off this way because they are speaking about something they truly believe in. The same is true with sales – be genuinely passionate about the product you represent.

It's genuine, it's real, and it shows. It's those individuals that have the most success in sales (you also need to have a strong work ethic, but I'll save that topic for another story).

Lacking that belief in the product or service you represent can lead you to come off as "salesy." As a sales manager today, I've led, coached and developed many different reps with different styles. The number one trait I see in high performing reps is a true passion for the product/service they sell.

It's best to perform heavy due diligence on the company you're considering making a move to. However, do not just Google them; there are many other ways to go deeper than that.

- Research the company and their competitors, understand the value props on both sides; this is who you will often be selling against.
- Reach out to current reps on LinkedIn at the company you're interested in.
- Reach out to reps that work for the competitors.
- Find customers of the company that you're interested in.
- Or a combination of all of the above.

Work backward instead of jumping forward when looking for a sales career at a new company.

31.

A RAPID RISE, AN EPIC FALL, AND GETTING "FIRED-UP"

By Scott Ingram

This is the story I was most afraid of sharing. I'm far enough removed from the experience now, and that trepidation is exactly why I felt like I should push through the fear and share what I learned from one of the biggest failures of my sales career.

When I joined Bazaarvoice, they were in the middle of a remarkable ascent. The company was THE tech startup in Austin that everyone wanted to work for. They had an incredible culture and were winning iconic logo after iconic logo on a very clear course to an IPO (Initial Public Offering). I jumped in with both feet and got off to an incredible start. I had the best first quarter any Sales Director ever had in the history of the company, qualifying for President's Club in that quarter alone. They changed the rules moving forward based on that particular feat. I was on top of the world and loving every minute.

That was our fiscal Q4. The next quarter, we hired over 100 people and doubled the size of the sales team, which was reorganized to accommodate the growth and create the new territories needed to support this new team. I won't go too deep into the details here, but I chose a team that was focused on a non-specific vertical that would serve as a catch-all for companies that didn't fall into the other sweet spot spaces where we'd been finding so much success.

I was with that team for 3 quarters, which was probably 1 quarter more than I deserved, given what happened. I learned so much... the hard way.

I have literally wrestled with what happened for years in an effort to own what I need to own and to make sure that I learned everything that I needed to learn as a result. The part of the problem that wasn't about me was really just about market fit. Generally speaking, this space wasn't a really great fit and the value we were able to deliver to so many other companies rarely justified the cost of our solution. The end result was that out of the 8 people that were on that team, only one person achieved their number one time over the course of those 3 quarters. We were 1 for 24 and this was a group of really strong sales professionals. Not good!

My biggest mistake was actually taking too much ownership of the problem and not asking for help. I thought I could figure this out myself, walling myself off and working my butt off to try and find a way through despite most of my efforts being futile.

Somehow I believed, for way too long, that I would find a way through and that everything would be fine. So when I was walked back to HR to be let go after my third failed quarter, I was actually surprised. I was so surprised that I hadn't worked on any type of Plan B outside of the organization, and had no other immediate job prospects.

Perhaps the best thing I did for myself after such an epic fail was to maintain a killer mindset. As I was driving out of the parking garage after being walked out of the building, before I called my wife to tell her the news (that's not a very fun phone call), I decided there and then that one day in the future when I told the story of my life, I would call this chapter "Fired Up" for so many different reasons. I knew the immediate future was going to be painful, but ultimately, it would lead to bigger and better things, even if I couldn't see what those things were as I exited that parking structure for the last time. I certainly was "fired up" after that. I can't say that everything went perfectly, but a successful career has many steps, and I learned a lot from this particular misstep.

Lessons Learned:

- You must believe in the value of your offering. If you don't, it's almost impossible to sell successfully.

- If you're in a sales role and you're not selling, expect to be fired!

- Nobody wants you to fail in sales. If you're struggling, ask for help. Ask your leadership, ask your peers, find mentors. Get help!

- Always have a plan B. There are too many potential failure points in virtually any company these days, and that is compounded in sales. Have someplace you can go if things don't work out in your current role, because you never know.

- Mindset matters. You have to continue to believe in yourself, even if your current situation causes you to doubt yourself.

- Get over it! It's easy to hold a grudge and blame others, but it's useless. Learn what you need to learn and move on.

- Win or lose, you have to continue to grow. Learn from the successes and the failures. I learned a lot from both in my adventures at Bazaarvoice and I wouldn't trade any of it.

32.

MOMENTUM SELLING

By Kyle Gutzler

In 2014, I was selling an HR software product that helped companies figure out how to properly compensate their employees. I began with this startup shortly after they received a $100M private equity investment. Despite the fact that we were rapidly growing and an investment group felt confident enough to invest a healthy chunk of change, from a sales perspective, it was flat-out hard to sell. Sales reps would often say, "If you can successfully sell here, you'll get hired anywhere." For the first year and a half, I stumbled around trying to sell this product and consistently found myself in the middle of the pack among other reps.

I desperately wanted to succeed. I clearly remember thinking that there was such a fine line between "average" and "wildly successful," and I was so close on many of the deals I was working. If I could just turn a couple "nos" into "yeses," that would completely change the game for me. Not to mention, the compensation plan aggressively rewarded high performers. There was an enormous delta between what high-performers were earning versus average performers... that may have been what kept me hanging around and pushing past the frustration. I wasn't ready to give up.

Toward the end of 2015, we changed the sales leadership structure and I was aligned with a new manager. I was a sponge and developed a few critical skills that really helped my sales process. In short, I began getting more bold and decisive with the prospects I was working with. I learned how to team-sell, where I would occasionally bring another person onto a call who would play a distinct role in the deal. I also became a masterful storyteller and had a bank of stories that I would pull from on a regular basis. Most importantly, I discovered the power of momentum.

As we neared the end of the year, I was consistently exceeding my targets and in one particular month, I broke a record for the most deals sold within a given month, which I would later go on to do again. By the time 2016 rolled around, I had a serious amount of momentum on my side. I set a stretch goal for total sales revenue for the year, which I didn't realize at the time would play such a crucial role in my personal drive and success throughout the year. In the month of March, I broke a record for sales revenue within a given month.

When you're winning in sales, everything changes. You start to become the person you really want to be. You say things with confidence, just the way that you imagined. You aren't afraid of rejection. You aren't afraid to say bold statements. You aren't even afraid to lose a deal, in part because you don't need any single deal to be successful.

Halfway through the year, I was well on my way to reaching my stretch goal. I had already qualified for President's Club and at this point, I was focused on keeping my foot on the gas pedal so that I could maximize my commissions and blow out the year-end accelerators.

I was promoted to a Team Lead position and I found a new sense of fulfillment in helping other reps find their way with sales. In fact, several reps throughout the year who were struggling with their numbers were placed next to me on the seating chart. Looking back at it, each of them completely turned around their performance, were promoted at least once, and all made it into President's Club. They began saying the phrases that I would say, sharing the same stories, having me join calls while adopting my methodologies.

The third quarter of the year for me was a bit of a struggle. I fell behind my goal for the year, but I didn't keep my eye off the target. My manager got into a routine of asking me on a weekly basis: "how do you feel about the goal?"

Come December, I needed some magic to happen. I had a few deals in my pipeline, but I needed one large deal that would put me in striking distance. For this deal, the VP of HR and CFO had both given me the verbal "yes" on my proposal, but the VP of HR said that the CFO determined they would have to wait until January 1st. For it to count as credit for the year, all I needed was a signature, not any payment yet. Even after explaining this, she said that because of SOX auditing rules, it would still be recognized as an expense for the current year and for that reason, they couldn't execute it yet.

We had some correspondence via email, but it was going nowhere. I always felt that if I could find a way to talk through any hurdles or objections in real-time, my chances would be exponentially better. I looked into every possible way around this, but couldn't find a solution. My best bet at that point was to get as creative as possible and try to get a live meeting and not necessarily worry about the solution just yet. I wrote up a thoughtful and creative email, with the premise being that whenever the deal was going to be executed, we still needed to review the contract and complete every other step. That way, when they were ready to sign come January 1st, they'd be ready to go, since they had an aggressive implementation timeline.

I got them both on the phone with our legal counsel as well, we worked through a few questions and revisions on the contract and sure enough, the CFO said, "Okay, I have no problem moving forward with this now." The VP of HR was surprised and even said something like, "Well, don't we have that accounting limitation through the end of the year?" The CFO replied, "No, that's not an issue. We can fund this right now." I was on the other end of the phone, pressed mute, and gave my legal counsel the hardest high-five she's probably ever received. The deal officially closed a few days later.

The lesson learned from this is that "no" doesn't always mean "no" in sales. Even though we're just talking about a timeline here, I found a way to have a meeting that was of value to them (not just me trying to be "salesy" to get a deal in before year-end) and we had a real human-to-human interaction, ultimately finding that the accounting objection was merely a slight preference and not imperative.

This deal put me extremely close to hitting my goal. I had just a couple days left in the year, so the clock was ticking. I had my famous scratch piece of paper that I had on my desk listing the names of every legitimate opportunity in my pipeline. I felt that I had several hot opportunities, but I wasn't taking any chances, so I aggressively went after each of them. One of my main philosophies at this company was to give myself as many different ways to win as possible. In other words, if I needed one deal to push me past my target, I wanted five hot opportunities in the pipeline that all had a shot to close.

On the final day of the year, I got into the office at 5:30 a.m. To say that I had a game-face on was an understatement. I had already well surpassed my month, quarter, and year, yet this was personal to me. I had visualized this goal every single day of the year and did not want to fall short. As the day went on, a couple of promising opportunities pushed, which was exactly why I planned the way I did. Finally, on my last call of the year, I got the green-light from a prospect. He said he'd be able to send back the signature before the end of the day. Knowing how sales go, I didn't want to run such a risk for me (or him) in having this push. I politely asked if he'd be able to complete the simple step (which takes about 30 seconds) to confirm the subscription. He replied, "you're right, why don't I just send this back now and get it done with?" As a result, it closed right then and there on the phone.

I can't even explain the overwhelming joy I had at this moment. After the call, I let out a battle cry of celebration and pure euphoria. Moments later, my victory song came on the loudspeakers throughout the sales floor: "What is Love?" by Haddaway. If you've seen the movie Night at the Roxbury, you'll understand why it's both hilarious and awesome. I officially surpassed my goal!

Lessons learned:

- The easy thing to do in your sales careers is to quit when the going gets tough. This experience gave me further validation that it's incredibly important to be resilient and push through adversity. Napoleon Hill even talks about this in his book *Think and Grow Rich*. To paraphrase him slightly, he says that success comes just one step after defeat.

- Setting clear targets and consistently focusing on them really works. It took me years to truly "buy into" this ritual.

I don't think it's a mistake that I came within 1 percentage point of my 2016 target.

- When you're riding the wave of momentum in sales, your confidence goes through the roof and you begin to tap into a level of potential that you may not have thought possible. If you believe this, then you ought to consider what drives momentum. My experience tells me that all it takes is one significant win. Knowing this, I now do whatever it takes to get that win, create momentum, and reach for larger wins.

- No doesn't always mean no. When working with your customers/prospects, you should certainly respect their decision-making, but I generally carry with me a sense of optimism, since I've seen so many initial "nos" turn into "yeses." However, you MUST believe this and at the appropriate times, giving your customer another opportunity to make a "yes" or "no" decision.

- Magic can happen when you get the person in a live meeting. I've found that email correspondence is never a good way to sway a decision. A live meeting reinvigorates the excitement and value of your solution, as well as the fact that a genuine human-to-human interaction is something that can't be replicated in other ways.

- Get creative! One of my colleagues says it best: "what would have to be true?" Even if your scenario seems impossible to work around, face the facts of your situation and think outside the realm of normal boundaries. The win that I shared in this story with the VP of HR and CFO was just one of many deals where I had to get creative and say to myself: "Okay, this seems impossible, but what COULD we do? What would have to be true to make this happen?"

33.

CAREER MOMENTUM

By Kyle Gutzler

What would then go on in the coming months was actually more meaningful. I decided to write up a post on LinkedIn called "How I Doubled My Sales In One Year." The shocking result of this article is it would go on to be one of the most popular sales articles ever posted on LinkedIn, especially one from an ordinary guy with absolutely no following at the time. I continued to find myself in a state of momentum. I had major publications reaching out to me, I was going on podcasts (my favorite, of course, was the Sales Success Stories podcast), and I was interacting with big influencers in the sales space who were endorsing my work, as well as many companies and recruiters reaching out to me who wanted me to work for them.

The most life-altering event that came of this situation is I was messaged by someone in sales management for an analytics software company. He said something like: "our SVP just sent your article to the sales leadership team at our company, we'd love to talk with you if you'd be open to it." After having a discussion on the phone, the opportunity seemed intriguing enough to discover a bit more. A couple of weeks later, he flew up to Seattle and took me out to dinner, where we talked at length about the position.

A couple weeks later, they flew me down to San Francisco to meet directly with the SVP. He and I had an instant connection and he was exactly the kind of sales leader that I wanted to learn from. After doing some recon behind the scenes in the following weeks, I spoke with several other reps at the company who told me that the simple fact of being able to work under this sales leader alone was worth it. Never mind the product, the company, or the position; this guy had a track record of developing sales superstars and leaders.

Nevertheless, there's always a catch. In order for me to take this position as a Senior Enterprise Account Executive for one of the most prestigious responsibilities they had to offer, I had to relocate down to Silicon Valley, a place where I didn't know anyone. This meant leaving everything. My family, my friends, my network, and a job that could not have been going better.

I had to ask myself: "what is it that I'm really going after at this stage in my career?" The answer was that I wanted to develop myself and push myself in new ways. I wanted to learn how to sell the biggest and most complex deals that exist. I wanted to go toward unfamiliar and uncomfortable environments and chase down my full potential. I wasn't interested in being a big fish in a small pond anymore. It was time to go into the ocean with the sharks!

I accepted the offer, sold almost all of my belongings and drove one carload of stuff down to a city that I had never even visited before. I now find myself in San Jose, California, right in the epicenter of the technology sales world. To share all of my learnings and development thus far would be a book of its own, but simply put, it was the best decision of my life.

Momentum is a real thing. Never underestimate the power of one single win. If you treat a win like it's sacred and use it as fuel for other wins, your sales career can literally transform before your very eyes and your life may not ever be the same.

Lessons Learned:

- One decision can change everything. Had I not chosen to write that sales article, I would not be in the position I'm in now, in an entirely different location, creating an entirely different way of life.

- Control your destiny. This personal testimony taught me that my sales career can be so much more vibrant if I have the willingness and courage to make power moves that send me down a new path and trajectory. My sales career is no longer happening to me, I'm happening to it and taking control.

- Change and get uncomfortable. This new experience has taught me not only how much development happens when you make a big change, but how many new things you discover about yourself through all of the change. I've found a new sense of fulfillment and discovered new things that I'm both skilled at and enjoy too.

- Prioritize your development. Your development as a sales professional is a bit like your 401k - you're investing in it for a brighter future. Your identity and value as a sales professional should not be wrapped up in your job. The moment your job is taken away from you, all you have is what you are. You should be fixated on building, refining, and sharpening your skills and development. That way, when things change and you make your way through life, it doesn't entirely matter what your circumstances are, as you've now developed an incredibly capable professional who is well-equipped to be successful in just about every environment.

I hope you have enjoyed my contributions to this book. Find me on LinkedIn at Kyle Gutzler if you'd like to connect – I'm always open to connecting with other go-getters. Happy selling!

34.

PERFORMANCE ENHANCEMENT PLAN – GOING FROM UNDERPERFORMING TO OVER-PERFORMING

By Mike Dudgeon

Playing Elton John's "I'm Still Standing" at 5 pm every Friday as a mini-celebration of my weekly career survival is not fun. Honestly, it flat out sucks. Big time. It's completely horrible. It was so bad, and I still think about this negative ritual every Friday. Early on in my sales career, my new Manager told me I wasn't performing, and I had 30 days to figure out how to change my performance. Now, mind you there was no prior warning before this and performance reviews were satisfactory, but nonetheless, I was walking the career plank. I never considered myself to be an all-star, not by any means, but at the time I was building a non-endemic misfit book of Enterprise business and still learning the fundamentals of sales in my third year.

When the news first hit, my emotions and mindset ranged from WTF, fear, confusion and, if we're honest, I was upset with my manager and blamed him. I took the weekend to continue my pity party where I hosted a thousand excuses to binge on my misery. I knew that Monday would inevitably come around, and I needed a game plan for survival. This one hurt bad, and I ended up sending myself into deep self-reflection and depression. I wrestled with fairness and truth for weeks. The fact was, my self-perception as a non-performer, and I needed to change the way I viewed myself to have a meaningful career. As I look back, I'm thankful for this period, as it placed me on a new trajectory.

"The two things in life you are in total control over are your attitude and your effort." – Billy Cox

My Effort

I was raised on a farm for a good chunk of my childhood, but for the other chunk, it was my single successful entrepreneurial mother who raised me. This is to say I matched the effort in hours, time and energy my parents displayed in their careers. My effort was there, but my time and focus were misplaced.

Sales Skills and Fundamentals – developing skills in your craft and mastering them may seem obvious. I believe most of us learn while we go and never truly master our craft in sales. In my case, I was winging it and doing my best to learn from others. In my sales experience, there was no formal training or coaching, so I had to learn on my own, and I wasn't doing that so I struggled to keep pace. I was working with a business coach already to increase my business acumen, but I then needed to master sales specific skills. I have read over 50+ books on selling and still continue to learn through blogs, podcasts, and other books.

Key takeaway: investing yourself by reading and practicing every day. Even if your company provides sales effectiveness training, you need to learn more, so you can differentiate yourself and be ready for more responsibility. Remember a CEO on average reads 50 books a year, and as sale professionals, we need to keep at the same pace. Sales Hacker's list of top 30 books is a great place to start (top1.fm/SHtop30).

Client Empathy – I had limited understanding when it came to learning that buyers ultimately need every business purchase to add ROI to their business, as well as their own personal career gains. I was selling a product I assumed they just needed. Therefore, on reflection, I was selling based on relationships and the brand of my product rather than specific clients' business problems. My new goal was to be at parity, if not better than my clients at marketing so I could actually be of use. I read twice as many books on marketing (100+ books on marketing and climbing) vs. sales to make sure I understood their problems and could help solve them. I believe the power of empathy sets you apart from the majority of sellers if you are able to provide a solution you believe in.

Key takeaway: ultimately, we are in service to our customers to help them solve problems and seize the opportunity. Learn as much as you can about their industry and their functions, so you can provide better solutions compared to your competitors. Adam Grant's *Give and Take* is an excellent primer to start down the path of empathy.

Balancing Relationship through Solutions – I worked hard on developing relationships by entertaining. I attended many dinners and happy hours with my clients, as I observed this in other AE's success and I tried to mimic their strategy, subconsciously trying to tap into the Law of Reciprocity. I believed if I did nice things for them, in return they would buy a lot of my products. This was true in the old world of advertising and marketing, but the environment shifted as ad and marketing technology provided more accountability and measurement. After reading Doug Weaver of Upstream's Oreo Doctrine (top1.fm/oreo), I realized I was investing my time and energy in the losing strategy of relationship selling. It was far easier to develop relationships, but I needed solutions and results to propel my clients and myself forward. I started a new goal which was to have a new idea every week. I was fortunate enough to have a process already in place from the experience I had gained at the ad agency (insights, ideas, and results) so it was easy to start. Once I did, my clients saw me differently and would call far earlier in their planning processes.

Key takeaway: ideas rooted in an outcome win, as the majority of sellers focus on product and relationship; have a process put in place on how to develop successful solutions; have a network of people who can help you bring ideas together. If you need a method, check out IDEO's CEO Tim Brown on YouTube and his TED talk on *Thinking Big!*

Risk – frankly, I wasn't putting myself out there. I was playing it safe by working with non-decision makers, and I wasn't challenging the real decision makers with my bold ideas. I was deathly afraid of rejection. Armed with my ideas, I challenged myself to make myself uncomfortable every day through outreach or sharing an idea with a client.

Key takeaway: begin taking little risks of making yourself uncomfortable every day. Tim Ferriss covers a great deal of this in his books, but you can also listen on TED radio hour (top1.fm/TF-TRH) where he breaks it down.

Communication – I was a nervous speaker who lacked confidence. This definitely shone through with clients and leadership. Over the last eight years, I've spent over $30,000 and, if I was to add it all up, likely over a year in practice time (with Dale Carnegie, Speechless, Toastmasters, online courses, notes on Ted speakers, books, YouTube, and podcasts). If I had to go to college again, I would major in Theater and Speech.

The reason I say theater is for the ability to practice putting myself out there in front of an audience with the fear of rejection and to get feedback. There is so much that goes into great communication (physical, non-verbal and verbal) that few people have mastered.

Key takeaway: learn as much as you can by putting yourself out there in front of others. I would start with Toastmasters or take a course. There are plenty of books to read on Goodreads for Popular Communication skills, but you really need education and practice. I spent too much time learning rather than taking the risk to practice my skills in front of others.

Communicate Up – again, I was not an over-promoter when things were good, and at the same time, I didn't share enough when I was facing problems. My leadership had limited knowledge, and as a result, I didn't lean on them for anything. This was the number one problem I saw in myself, and one that I see in others as a Manager.

When there are problems, communicate frequently and bring a solution. The experience that I have had with great Managers is that they know what to do, and they will be glad to assist in problem-solving and coaching, so reach out to them. Don't be a hero or be embarrassed. To this day, I communicate weekly in writing and get the problems out in the open in real-time, so they are no longer a problem.

You also need to market yourself when things are good. Managers are working with 6+ people on average and also dealing with demands on their time. You must differentiate yourself and set a brand image in their mind, your peers and leadership. I now have a cadence of communication to make sure they know I'm valuable.

Attitude

My natural disposition is laid back. I have a low resting heart rate, and I don't get overly excited when times are great or when times are bad. I'm what they call "chill." I also was okay with whatever happened to me as I felt most things were out of my control. When I had my "I'm Still Standing" moment, two things happened: I became obsessed with my personal development to be great, and I made sure I wasn't placing my success 100% on an organization or one person. I was going to control what I could control so I could improve my chances of success.

Obsessing over Being the Best – at the recent Sales Success Summit, Kyle Gutlzer mentioned the Kobe Bryant speech at the ESPN ESPY's in 2016 where Kobe said to other high performing athletes, "We're up here because of 4 a.m. We're up here for two-a-days or five-a-days." Kobe was saying it wasn't just skill and talent that makes them great, but working harder than anyone else. This was the same mental switch I had made and where I began sacrificing sleep, happy hours, trips, TV and other things I love so I could improve.

Key takeaway: you have to sacrifice a lot of things to be great. I've pulled all-nighters, worked through weekends and never feel rested. You can see Kobe's speech on YouTube (top1.fm/Kobe) and his English teacher's quote, "Rest at the end, not in the middle."

Being Uncomfortable – when I'm not uncomfortable, I feel exposed. I try to put myself in situations where I think, "how am going to pull this off?" I find these moments the most rewarding developmentally and professionally because I learn the most, but I also gain more in return. I would volunteer to speak at large client events I felt I didn't deserve to be at and to lead conversations with Executives I thought would never pay attention to me.

Key takeaway: Tim Ferriss covers it well, but the U.S. Navy Seals also express it succinctly in their saying: "Get comfortable being uncomfortable."

Extreme Ownership – this was the game-changer for me. However, it did take years to accomplish after my desperate situation. I had to take responsibility for 100% of my outcomes and couldn't blame others; not a client, manager, co-worker, my company or a product.

The first moment to begin my transformation of mindset was heading into a high stakes CMO meeting with our SVP of Global Sales, Mike Gamson. An hour before the meeting he said to me, "This is your production, and I'm only a character in the play. You must own it and be the lead character. You are the most valuable person in the room, more important than me or the CMO. If you don't own it, you lose all your leverage with the client." I owned it, and it started an ember in my mindset transformation.

A few years later I was reading Jocko Willinick's book *Extreme Ownership* where he says, "You must own everything in the World. There is no one else to blame." Something was empowering, not scary, about knowing I was on the hook for 100% of my outcome, but also concerning that I was giving my power away in the past. I started to formulate a different way of being an Account Executive, where I framed in my mind that I was a Franchise owner of my business. I was in charge of its success and also in directing the Corporation in what was needed to be successful. You can read more about Running Your Sales Career as a Franchise Owner in another chapter.

Each one of us works in different sales environments and have different strengths, weaknesses, and challenges. The one constant in your career, either as someone starting off, struggling to find momentum or crushing it, will be your ability and willingness to own your personal and career transformation. Transformation is, at times, complicated and overwhelming. Keep it simple by focusing on what you can control, your effort and attitude, and things become more transparent and manageable.

35.

GETTING PROMOTED IN TOUGH TIMES

By Paul DiVincenzo

I came back to Cintas in 2007 and, what I would call, a blaze of glory when I was recruited back by my Sales Director. He had really sold me to our new Sales VP in order to help me negotiate a great package coming back into the company. I had been a top-performing rep for about 3 years prior to leaving Cintas and still had a great reputation within the company. During my initial tenure within Cintas, I became a rookie of the quarter and rookie of the year and had achieved the Presidents Club in my first year selling for the company. I'd taken over a territory that was remote in the hospitality-heavy market of Palm Springs, California, and had made it a success despite the challenges after the 9/11 terrorist attacks. Many companies and hotels suffered with low travel due to fears of terrorism, however I was able to succeed despite the economic headwinds. I returned to Cintas in 2007 because the company had made plans to expand into vertical markets, such as healthcare and hospitality, and were creating specialized sales positions to approach these markets as opposed to simply having general market reps selling to all industries. I was told that I would be one of the next-in-line to become a major account manager in one of these vertical markets as soon as I re-integrated into the company. Alas, things don't always go as planned. In 2007/2008, the United States economy had the largest downturn since the great depression and almost every company, including ours, was affected negatively. Cintas had to conduct its first-ever layoffs, including the sales division. I was now set to be a local market rep again indefinitely. During this time, I had to overcome many mental obstacles in order to support my family and reposition myself to perform in a role that I felt I had already done, as well as figure out my strategy to get promoted!

My first step in this uphill battle was to mentally reposition myself and be grateful for the fact that I had a very good job during this hard economic time, as well as be happy that I had the know-how to do that job very well. *With the right level of effort,* I had the opportunity to make it into six figures in the worst economy since the great depression! Focusing on what you have to be grateful for has been a great methodology for me to overcome many challenges. In this particular case, I focused on how to maximize my income during this economy and what it would take in order to get there on a regular basis. I focused on the day-to-day and creating a successful routine for myself. This included prospecting, target marketing, and an extreme amount of activity so as to overcome the challenges of the marketplace (I had to present to 4X more prospects than usual to close the same amount of accounts). This would help me succeed in my current local market sales rep role and figure out a strategy on how to get promoted. To this day, I still look at my schedule and focus on Sunday night as my primary prep for the week. I would focus on what I needed to accomplish the next week, building a plan for that week and making that a consistent process that I could execute each week. This includes knowing what Accounts I wanted to go for and how I was going to approach them, as well as decision-makers and preparing marketing campaigns to approach those accounts. This consistent extreme level of activity during the economic downturn helped me to become number two in our region in the worst economic time since the Great Depression. I was also able to earn commissions and bonuses that allowed me to purchase a dream house in 2009 despite those challenges.

Great! I had figured out how to re-create value for the company, myself, and my family during this period of time, as well as a solid income. As with any top performer, I wanted more. As I was looking at the marketplace, I realized that Cintas did not have a focus on the largest, but one of the toughest markets... the government. The government sale is full of many challenges, regulations, legal hurdles, and a whole host of other things that our company typically does not like to negotiate on. However, during this time, we were looking for new markets to sell into which could provide us with new revenue. I knew how to sell in this very technical and bureaucratic space from another industry. I formulated a plan, as our executives were on roadshows coming to the local markets and asking the local teams what opportunities we see in the marketplace during the recession. Interestingly, in one of these executive meetings, they asked questions to the teams about what ideas the field had; most of the time, they would simply receive silence... As our executives came around to my location, I was prepared with five different ideas on how we could increase sales during the recession, one of those ideas being putting a specialty government major account manager in place to help drive sales in the toughest market. The reality is that government taxes are collected and utilized over the course of 2 to 3 years, so even though the private market was in recession, the government market was still thriving. Our executives were interested in this idea and asked me to provide more data and research to validate that this was a viable opportunity and that I was the right person for the job.

From the time I verbally pitched this in 2008, it took me about 20 months to conduct large-scale market research, provide complete market and prospect validation, and re-write my resume and sell myself as the right person for the job. I aligned with our local Sales VP to help in gathering executive support. Both our careers were now aligned with evaluating this new market and gaining corporate executive support to build out a budget for the new position.

The research and continued internal selling took countless nights and weekends away from my family to build a final business model. I'm not an expert in research, and thus had to do some research on how to do true market research! This included putting together many drafts and writing a literal book on how to sell to the government for our company and how that would look in our market including what projections, total sales, and budgets would look like. After a year and a half of selling, I finally gained approval that we would create this position that did not exist prior and was one of the first ever created by a field representative.

I was offered a salary and comp plan that I felt wasn't up to the level of effort that was put into creating this position. I did realize we were still in a recession, and pushed and re-iterated the level of value that could be created by this position within the marketplace and region. Ultimately, I was able to a negotiate 35% base salary increase in addition to the overall increased compensation opportunity, as well as the exciting prospect of building out a brand-new vertical within the company!

Lessons Learned:

- Never let outside forces impact your mental attitude.
- Always start from a place of gratefulness.
- You know your market better than anyone; know that that's your strength.
- Be prepared with great ideas at all times. Don't be silent!
- Study the problem, strategize, gain allies, be relentless in your approach.

36.

BE SPECIFIC ABOUT WHAT YOU WANT

By Scott Ingram

As you may have already read in my "Fired Up" story, my career hasn't always moved straight up and to the right. I've made a couple of wrong turns, which have been the most costly. You're going to make mistakes on deals, or maybe you screw up a quarter, but you can always recover from those mistakes relatively quickly. When you go to work for the wrong company, the negative impacts can last a lot longer. Hopefully, this story saves at least one person from making one of those wrong turns. Maybe that one person is you?

When you're looking for a new opportunity, it helps to be specific for so many reasons. First, you want to find the right fit for you that is going to move you towards your long-term career goals. Second, when you have that specific clarity, it's much easier to narrow your focus, because you'll know what your target company and target role look like. Third, it will be easier for others to help you in your quest because you can ask for exactly what you need. I used to speak a lot about networking and, often, told a story about being specific when asking for referrals that I think will be very instructive here. So here's your story within a story:

I was once at a local networking event. This was a lunchtime event where everyone gets up and introduces themselves. Over the course of listening to a few dozen introductions, almost all of which I immediately forgot, there was one great example of asking for referrals and one downright miserable example. Let's start with the miserable one. A chiropractor stood up and explained that a great referral for him would be "anybody with a spine." Seriously? That describes over 90% of the people that I know, but I don't have any idea which of those 90% to introduce you to. Shortly after, a woman stands up and explains that a great referral for her would be somebody who owns or manages a cleaning company, either commercial or residential. Because she was so specific, I immediately thought of 3 people that fit that description, looked them up on my phone, wrote down their names and numbers on the back of my card and handed them to her at the end of the meeting. People often worry that they're going to miss out on something because they didn't ask for everything, when the reality is that 'asking for everything gets you nothing.' When you ask specifically, you often get exactly what you're asking for.

Knowing all of this, I spent some time getting really clear about what my career goals were, and exactly what type of organization I'd like to sell for.

Here was my resulting list at the time:

- B2B Sales

- Technology, SAAS, Social Media, Services

- Solutions that target top-line growth: Sales/Marketing

- Large customer target market: $1B+ - Fortune 1000

- Travel < 40%

- A place where I could make a meaningful contribution and not just be a rounding error

- The opportunity to advance my career in the direction of sales leadership

The beauty of this list is that it not only guided my focus; it also helped me to quickly qualify opportunities. Not only that, but you can easily share it with your network and see way better results than if you were to send them your resume (which most people don't know what to do with anyway).

Unfortunately, to prove how powerful this concept is, I get to share a counter-example. After creating this list, I was a little bit more desperate than I would like to admit, something which often leads to poor choices. I got a great introduction to the hiring manager of a company, who will remain nameless (I've even removed the company from my LinkedIn profile at this point because it's so irrelevant this many years later). I had the skills to do the job, and based on the strength of the referral and my background, it was a quick and easy hiring process. Unfortunately, this role only fit about half of my criteria. I'd be selling to IT, not sales and marketing. There was no particularly clear ROI, and the solution would have absolutely no impact on top-line revenue or company growth.

As you can imagine, this just didn't work out. Fortunately, I was only in the wrong spot for about 7 months and I stuck to my criteria for the next role, which was a near-perfect fit. Had I been a bit more patient and stuck to my own rules, I wouldn't have basically wasted the better part of a year running in completely the wrong direction.

Lessons learned

- Define your career goals and aspirations in detail, both short-term and long-term.
- Make a list of YOUR criteria for the right fit. Where will/won't you be willing to settle?
- Ask for specific help and specific referrals, using your criteria as a guide.

Don't settle! Find what's right for you. It's out there, even if you have to take a step or two back, and pay your dues in order to get there

37.

DON'T FORGET TO ADD THE PERSONAL INTO BUSINESS RELATIONSHIPS

By Jelle den Dunnen

So, this is a bit of a trip down memory lane to one of the lessons I had to learn and still benefit from every day.

Back when I was around 20, I dropped out of college and decided to work myself up within a business. It was before the last recession and there were plenty of opportunities out there, so I applied for some roles and started shortly after.

I started in sales at a recruitment agency that provided finance professionals. My contacts were typically finance managers, CFOs, and the owners of accountancy firms, people that were at least twice my age and with a lot more experience and education than I had at the time. As such, I wanted to really come across as a professional, so I made sure I communicated very professionally. I always looked sharp; suit, tie and all that, and of course, I did some research to make sure I was comfortable discussing the topics they spoke about and come across on a daily basis.

I was doing just fine, but it was not until 3 years later that I forgot to really utilize one of the most important USPs that everyone has… that I forgot to sell… me.

It was due to my focus on looking like a professional and coming across like one that I forgot to show enough of me.

People buy from people, we all know that, but it's something that is so easy to just ignore because you're just doing your thing. It's not the first thing you think of when you're looking to improve your performance. It's not something you can get by running data analysis or anything else.

I can tell you that I also didn't agree to it when my manager at the time confronted me with it; maybe that had something to do with the way he communicated, but when my next manager also raised the point that I showed only a little of Jelle in my business relationships, it made me think.

I was very focused on not coming across as a youngster in order to be treated as a professional, but what was I thinking? Of course, they had seen that I was in my early twenties. Ok, perhaps they appreciated the effort that I put into coming across as a professional, but I was really showing too little of my personality and who I was beyond the suit. I wasn't fully utilizing the opportunity for them to get to know me and to get them to buy more easily from me, as they liked me for who I am.

It wasn't a change I made overnight, but I've become a strong believer over the years that you should really show a lot of yourself in a business relationship.

This is especially true if you aren't in transactional sales like myself, as my sales cycles typically last anywhere between 4-12 months. Therefore, you are spending quite a lot of time with your contact in these long sales cycles, so it makes it so much easier to build a relationship if they know who you are beyond your job title and the company that you represent. When you are working together for such a long time, it comes across so much more natural if you're just being yourself.

With social media and all the different communication tools that are out there, it's so easy to show and share who you are, but also to change the way that you communicate with the people around you.

This means that it has become so much easier to show yourself and get people to know you. Social Media and Social Networking are ways of showing off what your personal brand represents. Some people mostly talk business at networking events or on social media, but if you do that, you're not standing out from the crowd. It's not easy, but give it a try!

Someone from my network once said that if someone follows you on social media or looks you up online, there should be 5 things that a person should be able to recognize or know about you. 5 themes that you talk about more frequently, so when you get into a conversation with them, it's easy for them to grasp any of these 5 items. However, among these 5 items, only 2 should be work-related and 3 themes should be personal things.

Now, it doesn't have to be that black and white. The important essence is that A, your personal (online) brand should exist out of recurring themes that are recognizable and B, you should talk more about who you are, how you are spending your free time, and what your interests are, rather than merely talking about work.

A couple of items about me that are easy to recognize from who I am offline and online are as follows:

- I love traveling all over the world and I try to take as many holidays as my work allows me to. As such, I'm also counting the airports that I've flown from and, of course, I have a few travel goals to hit, haha.

- Skiing. Ever since my first trip when I was 16, I was hooked. I've never missed a year since, and when I can, I make more than one trip a year. There's just something about the beauty of mountains in the snow and the cold wind in your face when you're going down a slope and the atmosphere on a ski-trip or in a bar in the afternoon.

- My cats, Jack & Whiskey. There's no hiding from it. I think my cats are cool and weird. Mostly weird haha.

- Enjoying a beer in the sun. Whether it's at a nice festival, on a terrace with friends, or just with my fiancée whenever we feel like it… it's nice to be outside, relaxed, and living a little!

Anyway, enough about me. Back to making your relationships personal and showing who you are from the first moment that you interact with someone.

I mean, if people don't like you that much, they are less likely to buy from you, so why wait to get that out in the open? I would rather get it out on the table as fast as possible. Shit happens, not everyone can like you.

The other way around, if they do like who you are, it can be very beneficial to start building that relationship sooner and faster.

The more personal that business relationship gets, the more likely it is that they will share information that they otherwise wouldn't have shared. You're also likely to get more straight answers if you remove some personal barriers.

On the other hand, let's not forget about another important side effect... work should be fun! It's also way more likely that you're enjoying your job if you not only have personal relationships with your peers, but also with the contacts that you work with.

Now, I'm not saying that you should invite all your contacts to Thanksgiving and meet with them over the weekend etc. (some might come), but it can be in the small things in life. Share that you had a rough night if your kids were awake all the time, and show some pictures of your family, pets, or holidays. Share some stories of what you experienced as an individual, such as in sports or anything else you have in common. They are people too; the quicker you make these relationships personal, the easier it gets to find common interests or things that you appreciate in life.

One of the things I've actively started doing is just pro-actively sharing what I did last weekend or the last holiday, or what I'm doing next weekend or the next holiday. Everyone enjoys free time, and if you share something about your spare time, it's more likely they will share something with you about what they do after work as well.

Another thing that I started doing more is video calls. It's so easy to just hide behind a (conference) phone or e-mail. However, the best relationships are built face to face, so why not make scheduled calls a little bit face to face as well? This isn't just concerning relationships with external people, but also with your peers!

I can wholeheartedly say that I'm glad I learned this lesson. I've met some great people over the years and because of those relationships that we've built together, I've met many people as peers, contacts, partners etc. that I consider friends. Some of them have even become mentors to me as well.

So this story really is about a lesson that I wanted to share with all the younger people that are starting their careers, although you may have been working for some years now. It's good to be mindful that you're participating in a professional environment, but never forget to show who YOU are. So much good can come from it, both business-related and personally.

38.

BEST PRACTICES VS. ONLY PRACTICES

By Paul DiVincenzo

Many of these terms should sound familiar to you if you've been in sales or business for any length of time…. Let's see if you recognize some of them: best practices, role plays, phone block, activity, leaderboards, KPIs. I have been lucky enough to be a top seller in two Fortune 500 companies over the past 15 years of my sales career. Every day, I have someone ask me what my Best Practices are for prospecting, selling, managing my numbers, career matters, etc... I usually let them know it's not that easy and that they should focus on the fundamentals for now. Recently, I've been thinking about what I do that really does make a difference. Obviously, my sales success has come with a lot of hard work and with that, some great recognition internally at the companies I've worked for. It's interesting to watch the same lingo go around and around, mostly by sales leadership and, in many cases, businesspeople in general.

The one that stands out to me which offers a significant improvement for people that are looking to excel in sales is best practices… The reality of sales is that if you stick to the standards of activity, follow up, professionalism, and great manners, you should be *pretty successful*. However, if you really want to go from average to being consistently at the top, it takes creating something called "only" practices. This means creating significant differences between what ONLY YOU can or will do for the customer and the sale. It will push you ahead of your internal and external competition for sustained success. I can't remember where I heard this term originally, but when I did, I knew right away that's exactly how I've been in the top 10% year over year for almost 17 years. I didn't know what I did differently from any other salespeople for many years. However, after thinking about it, the short answer is that I am willing to do more for my customers than anybody else every time to exceed my numbers and make as much money as possible for me and my family.

When I first started in sales at the Cintas uniform sales division, I took over a territory in the Palm Springs California market which was heavily driven toward hospitality. This includes many hotels and resorts. I focused primarily on selling customers uniforms as a service; this means that the company rents uniforms for their employees vs. purchasing them. We pick up and deliver uniforms each week, as well as wash, clean, inspect, and repair or replace them to a condition that is wearable and acceptable in a hotel environment. Many of these hotels are 4-5 star resorts. This service has a lot of attention to detail and the back end of the business is highly standardized. In other words, we have a very small and limited selection of uniforms, compared to the purchase options, and when it comes down to design elements such as color patterns, there weren't a lot of options. It's a bit of a joke in the industry, however, it's really true, as you can only carry so many colors and maintain that inventory at a profit level that makes sense. I was selling to the Hyatt Grand Champion resort in the Indian Wells area of Palm Springs California. Although they had some maintenance people that would wear our standard uniforms, I was told by the Director of Rooms that the housekeeping department (typically a purchase-only program) wanted to chat with me, as they wanted to wear dresses with matching aprons along with a Hawaiian pattern that needed to be sewn into the garment to match some of the decor in the hotel. By the way, they didn't want to purchase it; they wanted to rent it and have me offer it as a uniform as a service…! As I heard the customer describe what they wanted, I almost fell out of my chair, because this was unheard of in our industry. There were so many hurdles that I simply didn't know where to start; however, the total opportunity in the sale could cover my sales number for just under a full year of sales. Because I was in such shock, it was actually a positive in the strategy. I didn't talk at all during the meeting; I simply listened, took notes and let the general manager of the Hyatt know that I would find a way to make this happen. His eyes lit up when I said that, because later I found out he had met with every other uniform company in our area, including a rep from Cintas, that all said no just as quickly as I said I would find a way to make it happen. We shook hands and I left the office, almost passing out in the 115° heat in the Coachella Valley area of Palm Springs. This project was so far outside the norm that I didn't know how I would get it done. It included learning about sourcing garments from across the country and outside the country, working with designers to have a pattern made, and gaining consensus internally that our company would produce this garment with a sufficient enough quantity for us to rent it (I didn't know any of this at the time).

I called my sales manager and let him know we had an opportunity to close one deal that could cover almost my full year of sales quota/ projections and that it was going to take something extraordinary for us to get it. He didn't have a clue what was about to happen. I went home that evening to my newborn son, who was only about 2 ½ years old at the time, and I thought to myself, *you have to make this happen, you will make this happen, you will find a way.*

In the following weeks after the meeting, I began to educate myself on all the capabilities of Cintas beyond my day-to-day selling job. I investigated what our supply chain opportunities were, where the dress was being manufactured, how long it took for the dress to be manufactured, and how much fabric it would take to create the trim and all the other elements. However, I had no clue what they were prior to that meeting. I had conference calls with designers, conference calls with manufacturing, conference calls with distribution and maintained engagement with those people, letting them guide me with their expertise. As I went through this process, I gained significant experience beyond what I would normally garner and have been able to use that knowledge for over a decade after that for sale in many other sales. This knowledge has allowed me to stand out from anybody inside my company or from competition about this particular category of our business. I didn't know at the time, but this is a key component to my overall success in not hesitating to jump in and learn a significant amount of information beyond my normal job scope, which will create a unique expertise for me that I can offer as value to my potential customers and current customers. Pushing yourself into the unknown is the best way to create "only" practices for yourself that you can then have for future use against your competition.

After my month-long education in the garment business, I was able to gather up all the information necessary to put together a business model, present that internally at Cintas, and create a pricing structure that didn't exist prior to the sale. I then went to the customer and was able to explain to them all the elements going into their production model, including hard goods design elements, and tie that back into how they wanted their resort to stand out from the vision created by the general manager. They didn't hesitate when I proposed a custom pricing structure that ended up being *four times higher* than any other program in the marketplace. I had delivered as promised. They approved it within two weeks including a multiyear agreement for services. I made Presidents Club my first year with Cintas that year, as well as rookie of the quarter and rookie of the year. That singular experience created a foundation of "doing whatever it takes" that I have utilized consistently in hundreds of other sales over the course of my 15+ year career with the company. This has helped me earn Presidents Club and Diamond Level recognition for multiple years and has allowed me to be fearless when it comes to looking into the future, creating something new and highly valuable for the company and my customers. Every day I'm creating, looking, and executing on only practices. By using this strategy consistently, I have been able to uncover new markets for the company, create new positions for myself within the company, and gain promotions and salary increases over the course of my career that other people have not been able to accomplish. This has not only allowed me to be in the top-selling rankings in my company; this has also allowed me to be viewed by the executives as a leading contributor to the growth of the organization.

Lessons Learned:

- Never lower your or the customers' expectations.

- Say Yes and figure it out for the customer.

- This will push you to learn more.

- By learning more and being resourceful you'll gain experience, tools, and resources which you can re-use to leapfrog your competition (other reps and competitors).

- Create and track your "only" practices from these experiences and push to expand those so that you will be offering experiences, knowledge, expertise, and the ability to execute on it where your competition will still be speaking features, benefits, and lower pricing.

39.

RUN YOUR SALES CAREER LIKE A FRANCHISE

By Mike Dudgeon

The first job that I had straight out of college was as a Media Strategist at DDB working on the McDonald's account. I was loving it! They even supplied me with a degree from Hamburger University, and I was fortunate for the opportunity. No matter what your personal feelings are when it comes to McDonald's, you have to remember that it has been a consistent business performer for the Corporation and franchise owners since it started in 1955. The successful partnership I observed over the years between the two functions (Corporation and Franchise owners) is how I eventually modeled my sales career with my company. I observed business savvy franchise owners who positively challenged the corporation through collaboration to better their product and company. In turn, this led to them ultimately gaining ROI from their investment. As I began my fourth year in sales, it clicked to me that I had an opportunity to think like a franchise owner to better collaborate with my company and have better control my personal ROI.

You are a Franchise Owner

You may not recognize it, but you are an investor in your company. The parallel I had drawn between franchise ownership and sales came down to investment in capital. Franchise owners invest financial capital for a return on investment. As sales professionals, you also make a significant investment, which is in the form of your time and talent. Some could argue that financial capital is more significant, but I believe that time is our most precious commodity and talent is the number one priority across many companies. Net: our time and talent are valuable, and we need to maximize the return. Once I recognized I was an owner, it was about moving beyond just short-term gains of commissions to include longer-term gains of experience and skills, which would compound over time for significant returns and greater control of outcomes. I also valued the professional relationships, working with people and managers I could grow from so I could maintain a consistent working environment.

As Sellers We Want It

Fundamentally, I believe all employees and sellers want a greater share of ownership. Looking back at the NBA Golden State Warriors in 2018, the team was given the opportunity to coach a game against the Phoenix Suns during the regular season. Steve Kerr, the Head Coach of Golden State, provided coaching opportunities for three of his players. The players coached during time-outs, the shoot-around and to break down film for the players. The Warriors won 129-83.

Steve Kerr said after the game, *"It's their team. I think that's one of the first things you have to consider as a coach,"* Kerr said. *"They have to take ownership of it. As coaches, our job is to nudge them in the right direction, guide them, but we don't control them. They determine their own fate. I don't feel like we've focused well the past month, and it just seemed like the right thing to do. I thought they communicated really well together and drew up some nice plays, and it was a good night for the guys."*

I see the same values and mentality in the sales Account Executives on our team wanting to own more and companies finding ways to give more ownership to employees. Not surprisingly, according to a LinkedIn study on What it Takes to be a CEO, sales is one of the top functions where CEOs begin their careers.

Action item: look around and see if you can recognize a mind-shift among your peers and friends in sales.

It's Already Happening

At Microsoft, you see where sellers are taking on more of the value delivery for their Cloud division. Amy Hood, Microsoft CFO, said in Microsoft's quarterly earnings in Q2 2018 when talking about their sales team, "And what we did was really fundamentally change how we go to market for all customer types. At the high end that's meant adding a lot of resources that are technical. And when I say technical I mean you would probably not see the distinction between them (sellers) and someone that works in Redmond writing lines of code that's shippable. They are fully capable of implementing and doing most project startup costs—costs meaning efforts—they're capable of getting projects off the ground, and they're capable of demoing all deep Azure functionality."

What's remarkable about this is, in a business, you (1) find a problem, (2) build a solution, (3) market the solution, (4) sell the solution, (5) deliver value and (6) account for revenue. You can see Microsoft sellers taking on more of the value delivery like a franchise owner.

A similar shift happened over 10 years ago in ad sales when Doug Weaver from Upstream developed a concept called Oreo Doctrine, where the sellers in my industry needed to add more value (relationships, skills, ideas outside of what your product offers and business development) to their client's problems.

Action item: focus on increasing your general business acumen to stay relevant as responsibilities shift and to control your outcome. Josh Kaufman's *Personal MBA* is a great place to start.

Let's get Started

Mentally Invest your Capital

You must make the mental shift that you are now an owner. It is important to remember that your investment of time and talent is just as meaningful as the risk of putting a substantial amount of financial capital on the line. I personally printed out a certificate of ownership to help make it significant to me.

Action item: share with a loved one or sign a document that you are now a franchise owner. You can also watch Will Jenkins talk about time to understand the power of time.

Mentally Take Ownership and Leadership

As an owner, you are now a leader and must take full responsibility for all outcomes. What I witnessed among the franchise owners was a mindset that ultimately, they were on the hook for results. You will need to do the same with no blame to the product, client, teammates, partners, etc. In Jocko Willink's book *Extreme Ownership*, he says, "Leaders must own everything in their world. There is no one else to blame." You must prepare yourself to solve problems and grasp the opportunity.

Action item: strive to reduce the amount of blame on others and be okay with only controlling what you and your team can control.

Trust the System

McDonald's is disciplined in the processes of being consistent in delivering value to its customers. We need to do the same with leaders creating procedures to follow. My Director has six pillars of success we follow, and I tend to follow them doggedly. I have three additional pillars to achieve success with my book of business, but will only act on them if my Director agrees. Another key quote in Jocko's book that I love is, "Discipline equals freedom." Freedom opens up time, and new doors so trust the process.

Action item: ask your leader what their operating principals are and share your ideas with him/her as well to receive feedback.

Collaborate with Others

You need to be able to influence internally within your organization to best serve your clients and improve your overall product. To do so, you need to be likable, share ideas and solutions. Gone are the days you command respect by being loud, by complaining or expecting others to solve problems for you. You must observe opportunities and issues that need to be solved and share the potential solutions.

Action item: to best collaborate, you need to improve your knowledge of other functions, develop relationships and sell ideas to others.

Josh Kaufman in his *Personal MBA* book, shares- there are five parts to every business (Value Creation, Marketing, Sales, Value Delivery and Finance) which is a great framework that can work internally. Great franchise owners are fluent in all five, and I believe AEs should have a general understanding of the five.

- Value creation – get to know your product team and provide feedback from the field on what customers need and how to differentiate from competitors.

- Marketing – in LinkedIn's "Rethink the B2B Buyer's Journey," they shared from Forrester that up to 90 percent of the buyer's journey may be complete before they reach out to a seller. It's more important than ever to be in tune with your marketing team, but also to think like a marketer. As sellers, we need to develop relationships with our marketers and participate more.

- Sales – continue to master your skills, but also invest in relationships with your sales leadership.

- Value delivery – your reputation is on the line in when it comes to what is being delivered. You must ensure the product being delivered matches the expectations you set.

- Finance – this is an area that can hold up your deals and you want to be as close to these folks to make sure deals are done quickly.

Giving Back

McDonald's franchise owners were always giving back to their communities, but they also provide new ideas to the corporation. It created a virtuous cycle of positivity and value creation. I willingly will give time to others and to the Org. It allows me to develop new skills, but I also recognize that it improves our overall business. These do not have to be big initiatives but rather the projects that are meaningful to you and to the company. I have developed new narratives, challenged product with new products and mentored younger AEs. Find the time to give back; your work will become more meaningful, and others will see how much you care.

Action item: seek out and ask for a smaller project to volunteer on.

Grow the Brand of You

With all the value you are providing, it's meaningless unless others know about it. One of my biggest dings in performance reviews was, "You're doing great things, but nobody knows about it." Find a natural way to share all the great things you do. Don't force it though. I maintain a calendar of meetings with leadership and cross-functional teammates to understand what they're working on and what they might need help with. This creates an environment to share without sounding like I'm showboating.

Action item: keep a regular occurrence of meetings with key stakeholders to share all the value you're creating.

Treating your sales career like Franchise Owners provides many benefits to you as a seller. You find yourself more valuable to your company, clients, and self. Your confidence and skill level will grow and discovering confidence will help you compete in any professional opportunity. I look at Greg Flynn, who is known as one of the top franchisees in the world, as a pinnacle of success. He's not only made a tremendous amount of money but also changed the franchise industry. As sellers, we have the same opportunity to continue to evolve our role within our Orgs to maximize our success. Good luck on your journey.

40.

GETTING IT DONE & DOING IT RIGHT – RECIPE FOR A GREAT SALES CULTURE

By Scott Ingram

I've had the opportunity to work with some great sales leaders, and the best of the best was Alex Shootman. Alex was the Chief Revenue Officer (CRO) at Eloqua when I joined the company and is currently serving as the CEO of Workfront.

Since the hiring manager and my future boss for this role was based in San Francisco, and Alex and I were both based in Austin, I initially spent more time interviewing with Alex than I did with Dennis. In one of those first conversations with Alex, I fell in love with the sales culture he was creating after he walked me through his Getting it Done & Doing it Right framework.

Alex grabbed a notepad and drew a simple 2X2 matrix. On the left-hand side, he wrote the letters G-I-D, which he explained stood for Getting it Done. At the bottom, he wrote the letters D-I-R for Doing It Right.

He started with the upper right quadrant and explained this was the easiest. As he drew a star in that box, he told me that the sales professionals in the organization who were both getting it done while doing it right would be stars. They would be recognized and rewarded.

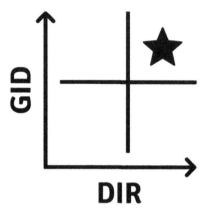

From there, he moved to the next easiest to explain quadrant in the bottom left, where he wrote a large letter F. He suggested this position was fairly self-evident, as sellers who weren't performing against either measurement should expect to be fired.

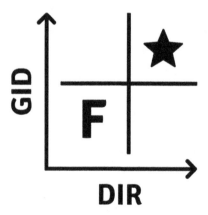

Next he moved to the bottom right quadrant where he wrote a large letter C. I distinctly remember him telling me that "We believe that good things happen to good people," and went on to explain that those who weren't getting it done, but were doing it right deserved a chance. The C was for coaching, and he believed in coaching and working with these under performers to help them improve and move up to the top right quadrant where they would be recognized and rewarded for their efforts as stars.

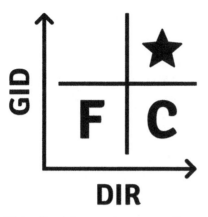

This all made complete sense. It was simple, straightforward and he shared additional details around what it means to get it done. For the most part that was about making your numbers. This is sales after all. Not to mention some of the nuances around doing it right. Things like being a true team player and working with other departments, putting customers and their experience first and doing what's right by them. But the real genius in this model came as he explained the heart of the culture and how the sales leadership team would deal with those who fell into the last quadrant.

In that box, Alex wrote the letters F-F and explained those who were getting it done (achieving or exceeding their numbers), but not doing it right, could expect to be Fired Faster.

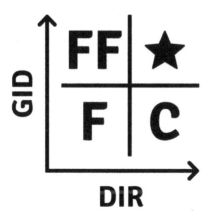

At that point in my career, I'd seen enough to know that right in front of me was the solution to the toxic sales culture. One so often dominated by an ultra-high performer who got to that position because they were all about themselves and would do anything to anybody inside or outside of the organization to get what they wanted. On paper they look like rock stars, but if you dig a little deeper into the real cost of their behavior, it can be extremely detrimental in so many ways. In a word they create churn. The deals they bring in will often not renew, and other strong sellers will often leave because of the actions these toxic individuals take. A couple of which are best described in Lee Bartlett's book *The No. 1 Best Seller* as 'The Leech' and 'The Confidence Trickster' and this is often exacerbated by the actions or more often the inactions of a poor manager.

Not only was this Getting It Done & Doing It Right framework a recipe for a great sales culture, but it also worked its way into the whole company's culture. Everyone bought into this idea, and the result was one of the most collaborative and innovative environments I've ever worked in. Most importantly, it wasn't just an attempt at lip service. We all lived these principles and once or twice I even saw leadership act on the fired faster mandate with a bad actor further reinforcing their commitment to this model and deepening our trust in them.

Lessons Learned

- Culture matters. Get to know an organization and what drives them before you sign that offer letter.

- Leadership matters, and it will have an impact on your results either positively or negatively.

- Talk is cheap. Look at the values that an organization actually act on. What they do matters much more than what they say.

Sales Process

41.

WHY IS WHY BETTER
THAN WHAT?

By DeJuan Brown

Linear thinking patterns. This is how I would best describe my sales approach prior to around 2010.

I definitely considered myself to be a "good" salesperson, achieving above-quota results for (at that time) the last 8 years.

Could I improve in some areas? Absolutely. I mean, who couldn't? I had a clear recognition that growth and development were necessary for long-term success. I did what I knew to do, and likely what many other sales professionals do, in order to get better.

I read books, I listened to my mentors and those who were successful around me, and I listened to podcasts. I found great value in all of these.

Yet, I felt like there was something missing from my sales process. I'd gotten better at asking good questions, and certainly at linking articulated pain to elements in our solution that could help alleviate it.

You know... the good old one-two-three.

1. What's your situation?

2. What is painful about that situation?

3. Here's how we can help with that situation.

At this point, my talk track began to feel more like 'rote memory' than 'discovery'... more like 'interrogation' than 'interview.'

Something had to change, but I didn't quite know what.

So let's visit the fateful day in 2010 when a colleague of mine named Jason.....okay, let's shoot for honesty here - Jason was more than a colleague. He was my sales idol slash arch nemesis. Seriously, the guy sold nearly 250% of EVERY possible quota, EVERY year. I just wanted to unplug his computer and listen, learning from his calls. I'd never been so emotionally torn in my life.

Anyway, Jason was super gracious. He was a virtual open book, always more than willing to help and answer any questions you had. This actually made it harder to keep him on my arch nemesis list, and it made me want to be an ally. Such a combination of humility and excellence tends to have that sort of effect.

So one day, I ask him how in the world he gets clients to spend 8x with us versus our competitors. His answer was shorter than I expected and more cryptic than I could comprehend.

"The Golden Circle."

"WHAT?" I asked with all the confusion of a 9-year old watching a Quantum Physics documentary.

"The Golden Circle," he repeated. "You haven't seen Simon Sinek's TED Talk?"

"WHO? No, I haven't."

"You should watch it; I'll send you the link." (top1.fm/GoldenCircle)

I've already mentioned my admiration (although I didn't call it that) of Jason, so as soon as he sent me the link, I dove right into this uncharted water.

By minute 5 of an 18-minute video, I was floored with epiphany after epiphany. My approach to prospects and conversations was about to change.

What I hope to share next is just one of many insights I gleaned, along with the baby steps I took in order to integrate it into my process.

People don't buy what you do, they buy WHY you do it.—This principle made me realize immediately that I had no "why." In the presence of a strong "why," there is a strong belief.

How could I convey belief statements that resonated if I didn't know what I, or my company for that matter, believed regarding the solutions we offered?

The baby step I took here was to seriously consider and internalize the "whys" of:

My organization

Myself

My Clients/Prospects

The solutions we served them with

Example: Why did we design our interface as we did? Why did I seek employment with this company to begin with? Why do we continue to innovate in the market in ways that benefit our clients?

My answers, based on my perception of Sinek's video, needed to be in the form of "belief statements."

Example: We believe that the layout of a tax program should align exactly with the steps in the workflow of our practitioners.

The early result of executing against this one-part strategy was a rapid buy-in from clients.

Honestly, you'd be hard-pressed to find a tax practitioner who doesn't believe the same thing about a platform. I was finding that the issue wasn't non-belief, but prior to my stating this belief, there was no frame of reference for the practitioner to align with.

In other words, this was the first time they'd heard this, and they immediately responded as if to say "hey...yeah, we believe that too!"

Sinek's talk taught me to move from this mutual belief, to "because we believe that, here's how we've designed our platform."

The outcome was amazing. From this one tweak in my process, tying belief to design ("Why" moves to "How"), and design rationale to the product ("How" moves to "What"), my conversations changed forever!

No longer was I involved in 'rote memory' or 'interrogations,' but real discovery fueled by mutual curiosity and beliefs.

I began, as an extension of this flow, asking prospects about their own beliefs and motivations. This would lead to really open, transparent discussions that naturally led to solutions which filled gaps.

What was really interesting is that there were times I'd make suggestions for solutions besides my own to fill some of those gaps.; this only served to increase my credibility and standing as a trusted advisor with my prospects.

It was from this position that they would seek me out for answers, actually hoping they could do business with me. Saying that these learnings were paradigm shifts would be an understatement here.

So let's tie this all together with an excerpt of how this might play out in a meeting.

DeJuan (D): Out of curiosity, why is it that you got into accounting to begin with? Did you have family in the industry?

Prospect (P): Not at all. Honestly, I really get a kick out of seeing small business owners win. I think at first I wanted to be a conventional entrepreneur myself, but gave up when the road started seeming impossible. I really respect what it takes to start a business and maintain it, so I wanted to work closely with those who did it. The funny thing is, pursuing my degree, I realized I'd be starting a business to help people who have started a business (laughter). So I guess you could say I became an entrepreneur mistakenly, out of a respect for those who became entrepreneurs on purpose.

D: That's super interesting. So is your practice exclusively in the service of business owners now?

P: I wish. This last season, I did get an influx of business returns, thankfully. Over the last few seasons, however, I've had more non-business-related individual clients than entrepreneurs.

D: Why do you think that is?

P: I've been thinking about that lately. I think it comes down to needing to turn a profit so as to keep my own business up and running. What that means is that I take on clients that don't really fit the mold that I set out to go after. At the end of the day, I have to, because they pay the bills. This leaves me with less time to market to and attract the entrepreneurs. If you can imagine doing 250 individual returns by yourself and, at the same time, trying to get business returns in the door and done—it's like quicksand.

D: Wow, that must impact your motivation for the work to some degree? I mean, you got into it for one thing, but find yourself at this point doing less and less of that one thing. How do you feel about your future in the business?

P: I'm really not sure. It is frustrating at times. When it's good it's great, but when it's not, I definitely consider giving it up. There are things I'm passionate about and I'd love to be able to pursue those interests with increased vigor.

D: Do you mean things outside of business that you're passionate about, or the aspects of this business specifically?

P: This business. I mean, I know in every job there is a percentage of time spent on things that are necessarily mundane, but that percentage does seem to keep growing.

D: Makes complete sense. That's not a foreign sentiment to me. I hear similar stories often in my world too. Still, we believe that our clients' tax software should actually perform like an experienced staff member. Have you considered hiring help to minimize your non-dream work? (We both smiled).

P: I have, but we'd have to get to a much more profitable state before that could happen.

D: Does it make sense to you that such great software could perform like a new hire? What are your thoughts about that belief? Do you think that's crazy? I mean, if it's true, it's definitely cheaper than a new hire, right?

Although some of the details of this conversation may be outside the scope of your industry, I hope it's helpful nonetheless.

I started by asking about the "Why" of my prospect, and as you can read, it led to a real conversation. During this conversation, which wasn't a "bip/bip/boom" format as my interviews used to be, I uncovered so many nuggets of great information.

The "spoiler alert" is that we continued to talk and, within a few minutes, got to a point of agreement around this belief statement:

"We believe that Tax Professionals should be able to generate profit without sacrificing the pursuit of their passion."

We ultimately earned this prospect's business, and indeed enabled them to maximize the time they spent with their "dream client."

This is just one example of how different my conversations with clients and prospects became after watching that video.

Not every conversation goes this well or even uncovers this much. However, it's this broad-to-narrow thinking that has informed my preparation for meetings and has deeply impacted my results.

If only 3 out of 10 conversations took on this sort of shape, how would that impact your results?

Speaking to and from the deeper motivations (the WHY) of our audience and ourselves eerily resembles the norms of human interaction. I think this is why it's proven to be such a powerful differentiator.

We are, after all, humans serving other humans. Subsequently, the more we listen and respond like humans, the more human our customers feel free to be.

42.

SET YOUR GOALS AT 2X TO 3X YOUR QUOTA AND BUILD A DAILY ROUTINE TO OVER ACHIEVE

By Trey Simonton

We all hear about the importance of setting our goals high, but I struggled for many years to understand what that meant, and how to create a plan to overachieve on my quota. As a seasoned sales rep, I've watched many of the best focus on their numbers. They dissect their territory well and seem always to have a plan to quickly exceed their quota, get into accelerators and make some real money. That's why we do what we do – right?!

A better way of managing this process became very clear in January of 2010. I had just attended a conference where Mark Allen, six-time Ironman Triathlon World Champion, spoke about his struggle to be one of the best tri-athletes of all time. Mark shared that although for years he dominated in triathlons around the globe, he continuously finished behind Dave Scott at the Ironman Triathlon World Championship in Kona, Hawaii. Mark shared that to be a World champion and to beat Dave Scott; he had to change his diet, training and focus to be the best. Mark's talk got me thinking that maybe I needed to step back and change my approach to sales.

When I returned to the office that year, we were in the middle of territory planning. Instead of doing what I always did, I took a different approach and scheduled a meeting with my sales operations team. I asked for detailed stats on my average deal size the prior year and the average deal size of the broader sales team. I requested conversion rates for how many emails it took on average across the team to get to one sales call, and how many calls it took with a prospect before it created an opportunity. With that information, my close rates were easy to understand; this helped me set weekly goals around the pipeline I needed to achieve my higher goals. I wanted to look at my sales activity as a math problem.

My Quota	$1,200,000
My Personal Goal	$2,400,000
Pipeline Required (4x based on close rates)	$9,600,000
Pipeline Required per Week (50 Weeks)	$ 192,000
Deals Needed to Hit Goal (Average Deal Size: $120,000)	approx. 20
Deals Needed in Pipeline (Close Rate: 27%)	approx. 80
Meetings needed to get to an Opp (Success Rate: 1 in 4)	4
Calls needed to schedule a meeting (Success Rate: 1 in 8)	8
Emails needed to secure a meeting (Success Rate: 1 in 32)	32

I took the time to back into what activities it would take daily to reach my higher annual sales goals. We all know that 4x pipeline is a good target for sales bookings. That number divided by 50 selling weeks helped me realized how much pipeline I needed to generate each week. Taking it a step further, my success rate for calls or meetings that turn into an opportunity was also one in four. As I dug deeper, I discovered that it took about 32 emails or about eight phone calls to generate one meeting.

Once I knew my numbers, I threw out any thought about my quota and created new habits and routines based on my personal annual sales goal. I have a wife and two children, so three days of the week, I got up an hour earlier and sent thirty-two emails and made eight phone calls. Most of the phone calls were messages, but I found prospects to be impressed that I was up earlier than they were.

The emails and phone calls became an obsession, but I believed in the numbers. I knew if I stuck with the routine. Eventually the pipeline would come. Early morning emails and calls required me to prepare the list of whom I wanted to contact and the messaging the night before. I even scheduled 90 minutes of time to myself every Sunday to get direction on whom I wanted to target and the message I wanted to share.

Over time, the pipeline started to come. I found that the way I spent my days was changing. I would have all my prospecting done by 6am before my daughter woke up and when I arrived at the office, my time was spent fielding client calls, preparing proposals and progressing deals. My productivity went through the roof!

As the end of the year approached, I was tracking towards $2.5 Million in sales. As often happens, a $300,000 deal pushed out into the following year, and I finished at $2.2 Million in sales – 92% of my $2.4 Million goal. Internally, I was devastated. I had changed my routines but failed to hit my sales goals.

Externally, I celebrated. I finished #3 out of 60 reps globally and made more money that year than I had made the two years prior. Further, I closed the last $300,000 deal in late January of the next year starting off my next selling year with real momentum.

I continue this routine today, knowing I must understand my numbers and set my goals high to be one of the best, for both myself and the company I represent.

43.

DIFFERENTIATING YOURSELF FROM THE AVERAGE SALES DEVELOPMENT REP (SDR)

By Florin Tatulea

Becoming one of the best in any particular discipline is not easy, but starts with having belief in yourself first and foremost. It sounds cliché, but this is much easier said than done. I'm talking about the belief where every ounce of you to the core believes in what you are setting out to do and no external doubt or person can influence you otherwise.

If you ask any single person if they think they are better than average, most will tell you that they are. The truth though, is that most people have a fear of success and only artificially believe in themselves.

The moment that a negative person or external circumstance challenges that belief, the self-doubt begins to set in because they weren't fully bought into themselves and their purpose to the core.

The fear of success is something I've personally struggled with; this stems from self-doubt in thinking that one is not special nor worthy of remarkable things.

The funny thing is that the average person, or SDR in this case, is really not that good at all. The things that consistently distinguish an average SDR from a top SDR are very minor things.

This is true in any aspect of life. Take tennis, for example, the things that separate Roger Federer from the 100th best player in the world are minor details. If you were to see Federer rallying with the 100th best player in a warm up, it would be nearly impossible to distinguish who was better.

However, the extra practice, the extra footwork sessions, and the extra morning visualization sessions add up over time to allow Federer to execute on the one point in the match that matters most.

There is so much noise in the sales development world today and prospects are becoming increasingly difficult to reach. TOPO reports that it now takes an average of 18 dials to connect with a buyer (Source: top1.fm/TOPOsdtech) and The Bridge Group reports that the number of attempts per prospect has risen consistently from 4.7 in 2010 to 9.1 in 2018, while the number of quality conversations per day has decreased from 8.0 to 5.1 during the same period of time. (Source: top1. fm/BGsdrmetrics)

This means that to break away from the crowd, you now have to be (a little) more creative.

Here are 7 (small) things you can do to differentiate yourself as an SDR in 2018.

1. Use Video in your Outreach

Although incorporating video in cadences is gaining traction and becoming more common, it still hasn't hit the mainstream. There is still time to use this method as a means of personalizing your outreach and standing out.

GoVideo by Vidyard is a free Chrome extension which allows you to record, send, and track customized videos to your prospects.

I have used GoVideo on a daily basis and have booked many meetings that may have never happened because I went above and beyond what most prospects had ever seen.

The content in your videos does not have to be anything revolutionary (if you want to be in the top 10%). Don't use a script; be your genuine self. Discuss a couple of points, showing that you have done your research, and use a verbal call to action at the end.

As an extra tip, I recommend keeping videos below 60 seconds in length and having a name card with your prospect's name as the thumbnail, so that they can tell it's customized.

If you want to get into the top 1%, you should go above and beyond. For example, you can create fully customized videos recording yourself singing a song for your prospect or tying in an analogy about their favorite sports team into your pitch and call-to-action.

2. Send physical cards or packages

Calls, e-mails, and social channels are becoming increasingly saturated. A good way to stand out in 2018 is by going the traditional route and sending hand-written cards, gifts, or sentimental packages.

Examples of packages we have sent include:
-Hand-written cards
-Edible Arrangements
-Cupcakes
-Toy Cars (prospect joked about wanting a luxury car, we sent it!)
-Company Swag

There are solutions in the market, like a company called PFL (top1. fm/pfl) which automates the process of mailing customized physical gifts through your CRM system.

Another creative thing to send is Piñatas through www.pinatagrams.com.

3. Cold Call outside of business hours

Analyze when the best time to call your ideal target prospects is and block that time out in your calendar. Typically, the best hours for cold calling are before the work day begins and as things are winding down towards the end of the day.

Being the best takes sacrifice, so figure out a schedule that works for you and wake up early if you have to. Stay late and bang out those calls. If you want to be average and are just looking for a way to fund your social life, feel free to work a 9-5, that's cool too!

4. Use Owler/LinkedIn/Alerts/Company websites to tailor your email outreach

If your prospects' replies are along the lines of "Unsubscribe," you are not customizing your emails enough. I have tried so many different approaches throughout my time as an SDR and the best results I have gotten have always been when I customized each touch point.

Ever since I eliminated template-style emails, I have received 0 "unsubscribe" replies and plenty of replies praising me for the amount of research/customization that I have done. The truth is that I don't do any kind of "revolutionary" research…it really only takes 5-10 minutes to craft an email that shows that you actually care, which causes you to stand out.

LinkedIn

Once you know which account you are prospecting, go on LinkedIn, find your ideal prospects, see if they liked/shared any interesting posts or what groups/interests they include in their profile. Also, go to the company's page and see what kind of growth they have experienced in the last couple of years. This could be a good indicator that they are in growth mode and most likely in need of solutions to help automate processes. Use this information and craft a 1-2 sentence introduction.

Owler

Owler is a tool that scrapes the web and finds all relevant news articles/ press releases on the account. At Loopio, we use Salesloft as our email automation platform and Owler is built directly into the platform. Owler allows you to learn about recent rounds of funding and press releases that talk about interesting product updates/events/awards happening within the relevant company. You can also use this information to craft a 1-2 sentence introduction too.

Company Website

You know best what indicators determine whether an account is a good fit. For us, the industries our prospects sell into are a good indicator. Therefore, I go on their website and look through their customers' page and find out what industries they sell into. You can also use this information to write a more customized introduction sentence.

Google Alerts

You can set up Google Alerts to get notified as soon as news comes out about certain prospects, companies, competitors etc. Use these alerts as potential trigger events to reach out to your prospects.

5. Send outreach emails on evenings and weekends

Similar to calling during off-peak hours, you also have a higher chance of getting opens on emails when the volume of emails hitting a prospect's inbox is low.

Most SDRs are not going to be sending emails after 6 pm during weekdays and on weekends. Take advantage of this fact and use your email automation platform to send your emails during these off-peak hours.

Try scheduling your emails **for 9 pm on weekdays or for 9 pm on a Sunday** when people are preparing for the week ahead.

6. Customize Connection requests on LinkedIn and don't include an ask right away

This, once again, comes down to sticking out from the crowd. Most SDRs are sending InMails and connection requests that immediately pitch the product/solution they are selling and have an ask from the prospect right away.

Instead of doing this, you should do a bit of research on the prospect. See if there are any personal/company milestones that you can congratulate them on without doing any initial selling.

Another approach is to have an insight about the industry the prospect is in and ask a question where the answer could set you up for a pitch.

For example:

Hi [NAME],

I noticed that your team/company is [STATE KEY POINT SHOWING YOU DID RESEARCH]. From my experience, that usually means that [PROVIDE INDUSTRY INSIGHT].

Is that the case for your team?

7. The purpose of a voicemail is to direct your prospect to your email

Let's face it, voicemail reply rates are *extremely low*. The purpose of a voicemail should be to get your prospect to open your email where you have your value proposition. You only have a few seconds of your prospects' attention at this point and there is no time for a pitch.

Here is a nice template I have been using recently, which was recommended by Tito Bohrt and works well:

Hi {{First Name}}, this is {{YOU!}} with {{company}}. I sent you an email yesterday about {{subject of email or topic covered}} but I have not heard back from you. Can you give it a quick glance and reply back? Again it's {{YOU!}} with {{company}}. Thanks!

This voicemail works because it teases some information and sparks the curiosity, which leads to the prospect going to your value-added email. It's important to restate your name at the end so that they can find the email in their inbox.

Lessons Learned:

1. The difference between the average SDR and the top ones are minor. However, minor tweaks over a long period of time lead to exponential results.

2. Always be looking to innovate; these 7 steps that work now may not work in two years. The important part is to acknowledge this and constantly push the boundaries of creative outreach.

3. In a world that is constantly changing and with technologies like AI coming into play, personalization and a focus on quality outreach will allow you to stand out and prevail.

44.

CREATIVE PROSPECTING

By Scott Ingram

I learned a lot from my time at Bazaarvoice. They had one of the best sales cultures, as well as company cultures, that I've ever been a part of. Though to be fair, Eloqua was way up there as well, and it's probably no coincidence that both of those companies had successful Initial Public Offerings (IPOs).

At Bazaarvoice, where we brought ratings and reviews technology to many of the most successful online retailers and brands, the way we engaged prospective clients through the entire sales cycle was really something special. We demanded maximum creativity and personalization from hyper-relevant outreach lead by our team of Market Developers (what the rest of the world now calls Sales Development Reps or SDRs) all the way through to new client celebrations. Importantly, these were as much about the client as they were about the sales win. We would often have clients on the line to celebrate with us as we hit a 42" gong and told the story of our newest client and how we were going to make them even more successful together.

This creative client-story-focused way of connecting was contagious and is something I've worked hard to bring to my own sales efforts ever since. Let me tell you about one of my favorite prospecting stories, as it was a ton of fun and I can also share the resulting photo with you at the end.

One of the companies in my northeastern US-focused territory was Steve Madden, the shoe company. My market developer, Alvie, and I had been trying to get through to their head of e-commerce with no success. Now, I can't recall exactly how we learned about this opportunity, but somehow, we found out that Steve Madden was going to be making a personal appearance at a Nordstrom's here in Austin. I knew we couldn't pass up the opportunity, so Alvie and I put our heads together and came up with a solid plan.

Fast forward a few weeks, as Alvie and I waited in line together on a Saturday morning for an hour or so for our chance to meet, and more importantly, get our picture taken with, Steve Madden. We had made a rather large sign that simply had 5 stars on it to represent the favorable customer ratings and the impact they would bring to the company's online sales efforts.

When we got to the front of the line, we asked Steve to hold the sign while we got our picture taken with him. He was a little apprehensive about what we were going to do with the picture, but we briefly explained what we did and what we were trying to do. This certainly wasn't the time for a detailed pitch, so he agreed to the photo and we were on our way.

We had a lot of fun using that photo in our subsequent interactions with the organization. I believe the initial response that came just a few minutes after we sent the photo to our targeted marketing executive was something along the lines of: "Well, one way or another, you managed to get a picture with my boss. I'm pretty sure I have to take the meeting now."

The image then worked its way into every subsequent presentation and they always enjoyed hearing the story of what we did to get it.

Lessons Learned:

- It's rarely easy to break through and get the attention of a cold prospect. Taking a creative, unique, and personalized approach improves your odds exponentially.

- Featuring a company's own brand (or executives) in your outreach can set you apart.

- Sales can be a grind. Be creative and have some fun. At the very least, it'll make for a great story later.

45.

THE ART OF PERSISTENCE AND KNOWING WHEN TO QUIT

By Florin Tatulea

I was in the office late one night, crafting an e-mail that was going to be my sixty-third touch-point to a specific prospect over an 8-month period. I sat there in the office, seriously contemplating whether I was insane for investing so much time into a specific prospect with no light at the end of the tunnel.

I knew that this account was a great fit and the competitive ex-athlete in me was too stubborn to quit. Then something magical happened; after 8 long months, I had booked the meeting which turned into one of the company's largest deals to date.

One of the most important attributes of a top sales rep is self-awareness and knowing when you should (or should not) give up on a prospect. Allocation of time is critical when you are dealing with hundreds, if not thousands of leads.

The majority of SDRs waste an incredible amount of time going after pointless leads, especially if you are in a smaller start-up where you don't have a senior leadership team or person responsible for identifying your target accounts.

Here are a couple of helpful tips I use to make sure that I'm being persistent enough to give myself a chance at booking a meeting while also allocating my time effectively enough to focus on leads that will turn into real opportunities:

1. Map out the buyer journey for an account

Mapping out the buyer journey is critical for two main reasons:

1. **The first viable vendor to reach a decision maker and set the buying vision has a 74% average close ratio** (Source: top1.fm/OVstats)

2. **There is an average of 6.8 stakeholders involved in a B2B solutions purchase** (Source: top1.fm/HBRnewsales)

You can start mapping out the buyer journey before you actually put a prospect into an account. Take out a notebook and start mapping the org chart for the specific department that you sell into. The easiest way to start doing this is by going on LinkedIn and searching for your end-user, manager, or director, all the way up to the VP / C-Suite.

As an example, a B2B SaaS Sales team might look something like this:

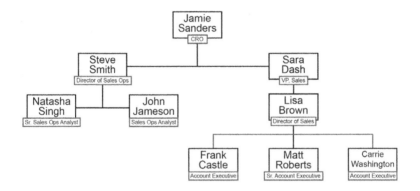

It's important to note that every organization structures their teams differently. Your initial map can be a guestimate and as you start prospecting while having conversations with different stakeholders, you can adjust what the actual structure looks like.

This type of exercise is useful because reaching out to all the potential stakeholders gives you a higher chance of getting at least one response from somebody. This means you can start asking questions to get in front of the right person.

It's also effective to be able to refer to the prospective colleagues by name because it sounds like you have done your research and are not completely reaching out cold.

2. A "No" is only really a No if it's coming from the person that can sign off on the deal

Don't get me wrong, it's important to build rapport with all stakeholders involved in a purchasing decision. Having internal champions and influencers at an organization can be the key to getting meetings and deals closed.

However, from a prospecting perspective, a "No" from an end-user does not necessarily mean that you should stop prospecting that account. If you get a "No" from the Director of Sales in the example above, but can communicate a good enough value prop to the CRO, they may delegate the evaluation down the ranks and you can be assured that the Director will have a harder time saying "No" to the CRO than to you.

It's also possible that the CRO will delegate the task to the Director of Sales Ops, who would be the correct person to lead the evaluation, instead of your initial thought that it may be the Director of Sales.

This is also why I typically like to take a top-down approach to prospecting. You have a better shot at getting *valuable* meetings booked if you can get the decision-makers intrigued earlier on, because they have the authority and knowledge of the buying process to delegate the evaluation accordingly. Your Account Executives will love you for it.

If your decision maker is saying "no," but an end-user or influencer is saying "yes," it's more difficult to navigate from a bottom-up approach because the end-user typically has less sway in the organization.

That being said, you should never treat the first "no" from any prospect, decision-maker or not, as the final answer, closing out an account.

Even if a prospect seems upset, take the empathic route; understand where they are coming from, acknowledge it, and start asking questions to dig into why they are saying no. In sales, the "no" and most objections are an opportunity for discovery and understanding your buyer's true motives.

I've had calls where I was told "no" three times in 10 minutes before finally booking a meeting. Get down to the underlying objection and challenge your prospects' way of thinking!

3. You must have at least 10-12 touch points in your cadence

The Bridge Group reports that in 2018, the average attempts per prospect was 9.1, with "high-growth" companies executing about one additional touch on average (Source: top1.fm/BGsdrmetrics)

This is important because you need to give your prospect a large enough window of time to respond. There are so many variables that could affect a response, including prospects being on vacation and bad timing with the end-of-quarter period, etc. Your cadence needs to be spread out over a long enough time period, so that the prospect has a chance to pick-up, see, or respond to your outreach.

In the past 3 years, I have seen SDRs trying to prospect into our team with an average of 2-4 touch points. I'm sorry, but that won't cut it if you are trying to become a top producing sales professional.

Cadences need to be at least 10-12 touch points and should include calls, emails, LinkedIn outreach, and video. If you want to go above and beyond, you can also consider using Twitter to tweet/DM prospects.

I can tell you confidently from experience that a large number of responses happen after 8 touch points and as mentioned earlier, I have even gone as far as having 60+ touch points over a period of 8 months to get a meeting booked.

4. Only go above the 10-12 touch point mark if there is some form of engagement from the prospects' end.

I don't recommend going for 63 touch points just because you personally think that an account would be an amazing fit. There is a concept of "diminishing returns" that says that at a certain point, you are doing more harm than good with additional outreach. For example:

1. You could end up pissing off a prospect
2. You could end up being flagged as spam by e-mail filters

Personally, I always look for signs of engagement with my outreach in order to make a judgment call as to whether I should continue or not.

Sales Engagement solutions like Salesloft, Outreach, SalesforceIQ and ViewedIt tell you when e-mails and videos are being opened. For the prospect I had 63 touch points with, I could see that the e-mails were being opened dozens of times and links were being clicked, so I knew there was some form of interest and that I shouldn't give up.

Lessons Learned:

- Mapping out the buyer journey in a prospective account gives you a better shot at getting a response, being relevant, and getting in front of the final decision maker.
- A "No" is never truly a "No" unless it's from the person signing the contract.
- Don't take a prospect's first "No" at face value; challenge their thought process and you will book the extra meetings that bring you into the top tier of SDRs.
- Have at least 10-12 touch points in your cadence.
- Be self-aware and only go above the 10-12 touch points if you see that there is some form of engagement in your outreach.

46.

THE JANITOR KNOWS MORE THAN YOU

By DeJuan Brown

I can't tell you how many times during earlier points of my career that I've prospected exclusively for decision-makers.

If I was targeting a CPA firm, I would only want to speak with partners. If I was targeting a corporation, I would only seek out the Director/VP/C-Suite inhabitants.

Don't get me wrong, the logic makes sense. Start the quest top-down. I understand wanting to speak to those with purchasing power; we know those as potential 'seats of economic power.'

There came a time when I wondered, '*Is this really the best approach for effective prospecting?*'

To tell you the truth, I didn't know for sure. All I knew was that I was getting tired of trying to penetrate the highest levels of some of my most coveted targets, only to make ZERO progress.

I was calling, emailing, tweeting and sending carrier pigeons; in some cases, I literally never got a response. Something told me that time would heal all wounds, and so I'd wait a few months then reach out again. Nothing.

If you know me, then you know that I have truly believed in and had a genuine passion for all the solutions I've sold. This meant that I really felt that if I'd identified a prospect, I HAD to have at least a conversation with them.

I tended to believe that my 'targets' were the only ones I could have conversations with which could progress, or even greenlight, a deal.

I began to try a different tact. Why not try to get a meeting with someone within the organization who didn't fit the profile of a 'decision-maker?'

We've all had those prospects that we were DYING to get in front of, but just getting into the building would still represent a win.

You know the ones I'm talking about. The accounts that make you think 'if I could just speak to them, I know for sure we could serve them well!'

One day I just thought to myself, *"Man, the janitor there knows more than I do about what goes on in that business!"*

I set out not to stop calling on those I perceived to be decision-makers, but to speak with others within organizations who were willing to meet with me.

Here are a few people I ran into that I would've never met had it not been for this mindset:

1. A receptionist who agreed to meet with me. She turned out to be filling in, and was actually a 25-year employee who had significant influence within the company.

2. A Tax Manager with 11 months' experience in his role. He'd been hired to leverage emerging technology so as to develop the business of the CPA firm.

3. An Executive Assistant who could offer me no information that seemed helpful (you didn't think it was a 100% success rate, did you?)

4. A Tax Attorney with the title 'Tax Supervisor' who told me, "Even though Rich has the title of VP, he doesn't make any decisions unless I sign off. If I tell him to go with you all, he will."

What's my point? Don't stop calling on the demographics that you find lead to high degrees of success in your role. Simultaneously, don't squander a chance to get into a building because you won't call on anyone else. There may be someone who is willing to see you.

We live in the age of the consensus sale, and even if you start at the highest level, few leaders worth their salt will make a decision in a vacuum.

If the CFO will eventually push you downstream to gain the approval of their direct reports, why not start with the direct reports to begin with?

For me, since the day I waxed philosophically about the janitor, if you will see me, I'm coming.

47.

ALWAYS BE A/B TESTING

By Florin Tatulea

The first time I heard anything about A/B testing was during my time in business school in my first-year statistics class. I always thought that A/B testing was pretty much only used for testing out different colored buttons on websites, seeing which would generate the most clicks.

Little did my 20-year-old self know that A/B Testing would become one of the most fundamental parts of my prospecting strategy in becoming a top producing Sales Development Representative (SDR).

To provide context – A/B testing is a way to compare two versions of a single variable, typically by testing a subject's response to variable A against variable B, and determining which of the two variables is more effective.-

Source: Wikipedia (top1.fm/wikiAB)

A/B Testing is something that marketing teams use heavily when building websites and lead generation campaigns, and it is something that sales teams are not leveraging enough.

A/B Testing is powerful because it allows you to make modifications to your outreach based on your own sample of data and numbers, not on emotions or general industry studies that others have done.

If you want to be a top producing SDR, It's crucial to run your own tests and not just take other people's tests as general truths, because there are so many things that could be unique to your company, target market, industry, etc.

Don't get me wrong, there is some value in aggregate industry studies for B2B SaaS sales, but if you are selling software - to lawyers for example - the most effective time of day to call your prospects might not be the same as a VP of Sales.

There is a large number of things you can A/B test. Here are a few:

1. E-mail subject lines

2. Time of day to make a cold call / send an e-mail

3. Wording in your e-mail body text

4. Calls-to-action

Here are a couple of important notes about A/B Testing:

1. In general, it works better for text-based outreach (i.e. e-mail / InMails)

This is because it's easier to control all the other variables and really test whether the one variable that you changed is making a difference.

For a cold call, it's very difficult to control all aspects of the conversation because it goes two ways and there are so many different paths that the conversation can take. Even if you use the same opening line, the reaction the person on the receiving end gives you can dictate where a conversation goes.

With text-based outreach, on the other hand, there is no opportunity for the other party to steer the conversation in a different way.

For calls, the only real effective A/B test you can run is to connect rates depending on the time of day.

2. You must have a large enough sample size so that your results are statistically significant.

Statistically significant is the likelihood that a relationship between two or more variables is caused by something other than chance. Source: top1. fm/statsig

Too many people make the mistake of drawing conclusions about what is more effective without having enough data. You can't simply send the first sample of four e-mails with one subject line and another sample of four e-mails with another and make a call from those results. Those results could very easily be based on chance.

3. Only change one variable at a time

The most important part of A/B Testing is making sure that you are only changing one variable in your outreach and keeping the remaining ones consistent. This way, you can be fairly certain that if your results are different, it will be based on the one variable that you changed. As a result, you can make a call as to whether you should move forward with the most effective option.

What should I use to A/B Test?

There are a lot of sales automation platforms in the market that provide you with the analytics and features to A/B test your outreach. The two most notable ones in the market today are Salesloft and Outreach.io.

If you are an SDR or Manager but do not have a sales automation platform for your team, I highly recommend you look into these types of solutions. They are complete game changers because they allow you to prospect at scale while providing the right amount of personalization and analytical/reporting capabilities.

Conclusions from my experience with A/B Testing

Please note that the results below are based on my specific target market, industry, and circumstances at the time. Although this might be good general advice, you need to go out and do your own A/B testing nonetheless.

1. The smallest variables can make a huge impact

Don't underestimate the impact of very small changes. I once decided to run a specific A/B Test on an e-mail subject line and the only thing I changed was making the first word of the subject line lower case. That one change increased the open rate by several percentage points.

I'm assuming this is because lower case subject lines are more informal and, thus, lead to higher open rates because prospects think they are coming from an actual person.

Test everything, even if you think it's irrelevant.

2. Use 1-2 word subject lines for email

I'm not going to reveal my favorite subject lines here, but most people overthink them. I've done a lot of testing on subject lines over the past 18 months and the top-performing ones were always 1 word in length.

1-word subject lines will stand out like a sore thumb.

Don't believe me? Go take a look at your inbox and see what the average number of words in the subject lines are…I bet you it's at least 5-7.

3. Call outside of business hours

Directors and VP-level employees are constantly in meetings or client calls from 9-5pm. From experience, I have found that the connect rates significantly increase when calling during the lower traffic times:

Mon: 4pm-6pm

Tues-Thurs: 8am-10am and between 4pm-6pm (best results before 9am)

Fri: 8am-10am (best results before 9am)

4. Send outreach emails on evenings and weekends

Similar to calling during the times with the least amount of traffic, you also have a higher chance of getting opens on emails when the volume of emails hitting a prospect's inbox is low.

Most SDRs are not going to be sending emails after 6pm during weekdays and on weekends. Take advantage of this fact and use your email automation platform to send your emails during these off-peak hours.

Try scheduling your emails for **9pm on weekdays or 9pm on Sunday** when people are preparing for the week ahead.

5. 3-4 sentences max for emails

Your emails have to be a maximum of 4 sentences. You should be able to include:

- 1-2 intro sentences which help you establish a connection and prove that you did your research on a prospect
- 1 sentence that "pitches" your product/solution
- 1 sentence that contains a call to action

It doesn't matter how complex the thing you are selling is; you have to be able to break it down into one sentence by understanding what your prospects' main problem is and teasing them just enough to spark their interest.

This 1 sentence "pitch" should have nothing to do with any specific features of your product/solution. Discuss high-level value that your prospect cares about (i.e. the actual business impact that your solution will have on the prospect's organization).

The art and science of A/B Testing

There has always been a debate as to whether Sales in itself is an art or a science. A/B Testing itself is the scientific part of sales, while the creativity to come up with new subject lines and outreach methods, as well as to consistently push the boundaries of what can be tested, is the art.

There is also an art that comes with being able to emotionally let go of your top-performing subject lines, opening lines in a cold call, e-mail bodies, call-to-actions etc. while you continue to test different strategies on an ongoing basis to keep improving.

As with most things, letting go is easier said than done, especially in sales where your results are directly linked to your compensation. Why switch your strategy if you are consistently hitting your quota and making money month after month?

It's simple – because this is about being in the 1%, and if you don't continuously test your methods, you will remain stagnant; moreover, if you are not moving forward, you are falling behind.

Lessons Learned:

- In order to constantly be improving your outreach, you need to consistently be A/B testing different aspects of your outreach.

- There will always be a better subject line - don't let your emotions get the better of you. Just because a subject line was getting you great results, does not mean that it will continue to do so in the long-term.

- Don't accept general industry reports for prospecting best practices as fact; there are so many variables that are unique to your circumstances. Trust your own data!

- Test everything; you will be surprised to find out that the smallest changes in an e-mail can have a HUGE impact.

48.

F*@# THE STATUS QUO
-DO YOU

By Phil Terrill

Selling technology can appear, to most, like playing in the Super Bowl or explaining Quantum Computing to your grandparents - it is high pressure and requires a level of finesse unlike many industries today. Selling at Microsoft may be even more complex, given our commitment to the cloud race and empowering every person and organization on the planet to achieve more. Our CEO, Satya Nadella, shared a powerful quote when taking over as Microsoft's third company leader in that "our industry does not respect tradition - it only respects innovation." As I started to reflect on this quote, I realized that executing against such an idealistic assumption would be more inspiring than I imagined three years later. Scott Ingram's Sales Success Stories podcast actually provided a fantastic opportunity to rationalize what I could not see so long ago by thinking about what made me successful as a seller at Microsoft.

F*@# the Status Quo – Do You

At first glance, given the above title, this may not be a welcoming part of the book. However, I wanted to be honest with you as this piece of the story unfolds. When I started my career at Microsoft, I was selling cloud services to small and medium (SMB) sized customers looking to make a really small, yet significant dent in our total share of the market. A year later, I found myself sitting at the computer screen in Fargo (North

Dakota) trying to figure out how I was going to manage a new territory and grow my $8,422,814 quota. It was not about the number or the 168 accounts, but the reality that Microsoft was investing in my abilities to deliver value back to the company by truly empowering customers to achieve more. After a little bit of time, I realized that the path forward was really simple – do you!

Now, before you keep reading, 'do you' does not mean just go completely rogue and forget you received a fantastic upbringing that embedded common sense into your DNA. However, in the sales game, sellers really have to figure out how to differentiate their value versus a predecessor. Customers really cannot stand the turnover associated with the sales industry, but sometimes, this is actually a positive moment for you to make an immediate impact. When I started my business/territory planning process, I realized that I needed to figure a few things out rather quickly that would help me to win and do it my way.

Run Your Business (or Territory) Like an Entrepreneur, Not an Employee

This might be the most critical lesson, albeit one of many I learned, that will ensure you are approaching your business the right way. Early on in the year, I had to figure out how to filter through the massive amounts of data aligned with each customer. I am sure you have to do something similar each year when assessing your book of business. The challenge at Microsoft is that there is usually a lot of data and a plethora of sources. To make it even more complicated, this might be the first time you have ever done this type of research. Treat running your business like you do your personal hygiene or finances. Each component of the process is critical, so take the time to learn your business. Many sellers think of this as territory planning - the time spent to meet your new accounts, assess gaps to quota, and then go sell to your customers. In the corporate space at Microsoft, I found my planning to be similar to running a business or building a new company. For example, think of a startup. Every startup or new business requires resources, the ingestion of capital, an intelligent plan, and customers. To help break this down, I am going to share seven steps that I leveraged to support my efforts in being a top-selling rep.

These few tips will help you make it through so you can start selling at a high level:

Step 1 - Evaluate Your Annuity Business

The annuity business is very critical, as these are existing customers on current contracts that are either providing annual revenue or have a propensity for greater upsides at renewal time. Take these accounts and relationships extremely seriously, as annuity customers have typically committed to your company's solution. That commitment could be an opportunity to expand your solution penetration into the account. In addition, these customers are great advocates or influencers to other prospects that you may be pursuing in your territory. Be sure to identify whether or not the relationship is strong enough to have that discussion, because it never hurts to have your customers talking to other customers about your great work.

Hint: *A huge chunk of my quota attainment resulted from high-growth and strong relationships with my annuity customers.*

Step 2 – Identify Gaps to Target for Net-New Deals

Gaps in your business research or territory planning may be very difficult to solve immediately, but knowing that they exist is critical. This type of information will help provide a direction to navigate when approaching customers. My process included identifying "white space" or non-annuity customers, evaluating current technology investments, understanding product utilization, and many other factors to help solve for these gaps. What became very clear was the fact that I now had a blueprint for success. I knew where recurring revenue would flow from my annuity business and now could visualize the opportunity in my business for growth. Net-new deals are the key to success in any sales organization. Pipeline coverage and health are important when forecasting over the course of a fiscal year. Consider where you can take a risk and pursue some big bets, which we will discuss in Step 3. These larger deals will be risk-reward scenarios, but will be worth it if you can pull them in on time. During my time as an account executive, my territory finished with close to 44% YoY growth (the business target was 30% growth) due to net-new deals.

Go after them relentlessly, as annuity business alone cannot help you hit or exceed your quota target.

Step 3 – Establish "Big Bets"

Now that you have identified your annuity and non-annuity targets, let's focus on the importance of "big bets" in your business. These are customers that you want to see massive change or growth for who have a high potential to close in the current year. This approach is about going very deep and across the organization in order to identify complex challenges that could lead to a shift in their processes or operational footprint by leveraging your solution. Identifying these opportunities can be challenging as well, but I will share how I simplified that process. Take an inventory of your largest customers, most disruptive related to industry, recent mergers/acquisitions or those you just really want to take a chance at building something special with as your targets. My best practice for each half was to target two or three large customers, through which I could drive "digital transformation" or extremely disruptive change that positively impacted the future direction of that organization, based on their technological objectives. At Microsoft, digital transformation is about partnering with the customer to build a long-range, high-impact technology strategy that aligns with their business priorities while favorably impacting their bottom line. Big bets are very risk-oriented, as you never know what the outcome might be, except a huge propensity to retire a lot of the quota while making a great impact with your customer. Take these opportunities to partner and collaborate with your customer(s), the outcome could be incredible for everyone!

Step 4 – Build an Account Relationship Map

Relationship mapping can seem like a very mundane or tedious exercise, but the payoff is tremendous. I am sure you are thinking about LinkedIn, but that is a support mechanism to a legit mapping of all the relationships that align to your accounts. The value is that you understand the players in your business. This exercise gives you the opportunity to establish awareness to influencers, decision-makers, advocates, time-wasters and anybody else that appears to have a positive/negative impact on your business. My parents always told me that "people like to do business with people they know," and that is what enables the mapping to deliver immediate value. The power of relationships and genuinely building connections with your business is critical to scale while generating influence at the same time. One of my early lessons as an account executive was that it didn't matter how much I knew, but how much I could build a rapport with people. It was about building a rapport or connection that was instantly received as genuine, so conversations leading to digital transformation could start to move forward. The other lesson is that with influence and a better understanding of the relationships in your business or territory, a better line of sight can be created to new opportunities leading to revenue attainment. Get started and stay connected!

Step 5 – Understand Business Priorities to Reduce Administrative Work

This might just be a pet-peeve or because I really found success in reducing the administrative noise in my day-to-day grind. I knew that without the noise, I could go have meaningful conversations with my customers. Building administrative rigor is extremely important as it relates to time management and utilization of energy. These two things should be put into "revenue generating activities" and not "non-revenue generating activities" such as excessive meetings or social time. When I was talking to Scott, my commentary on this was very serious. I truly wanted time to sell and not do administrative work. My process to achieve this was very simple – I asked my leadership what information was absolutely critical for them to make decisions and have a line of sight into my business. Once I understood those requirements, my pipeline hygiene increased, and the level of administrative noise decreased significantly. The ultimate results were that I was retiring quota and returning value to the company. Think about ways you can reduce the noise and you will have more focused time to build value with your customers.

Step 6 – Go Hustle & Win

Sales is a grind! Every salesperson I have encountered will tell you that if you are not hustling, you aren't eating. This step is simple – do what makes you great and sell! Each day I approached my territory or business as an entrepreneur and not an employee. I knew that I had already received my startup capital in that the company gave me a territory. That territory has value and my commitment was to grow that business. Each engagement with a customer was about providing a high-level experience they could share with a peer or colleague. I established clear deliverables and relationships with virtual teams (v-teams), such as partners or internal resources, in order to accelerate deal velocity in my portfolio. Running a sales territory is about agility and scale. Leverage the experiences, talents, and relationships of others to help you win. No one person can win the war!

Step 7 – Take Time for Gratitude & Self Reflection

The last step is about staying mentally aligned and managing your energy. This business is hard, and each win (or loss) requires a moment of reflection. Take time each day to recalibrate, so you can win the marathon and not just make it through a sprint. What contributed to my success was that I knew how to recharge my grind to match my desired outcome of being on top of the board. Think of professional athletes or anyone at the top of their game – they train their mind and bodies to be prepared for the whole game, not just a quarter. The other element of gratitude is being thankful to your customers. Allow me to explain this in more detail – customers are extremely critical in ensuring that you are successful!

Be aware of that and be gracious to them (and others) that helped you achieve a win. You will thank me later for sharing a non-tactical tip!

As you leverage these seven steps, take an inventory of what worked (or not) for your business. Consider how you can evolve and iterate against these tips to maximize the value in your territory. When you do encounter success, I challenge you to share the learnings with your peers and management in order to make an even larger impact. I look forward to hearing about your future successes as you learn from this book of Sales Success Stories.

49.

OVER-DELIVERING ON VALUE

By George Penyak

All top performers take risks; they evaluate the pros and cons of what could happen and take a very calculated risk. We evaluate time, where we spend it, how effective we are, and who we spend our time with. The following is a story about how I closed one of the nation's most well-known franchisees. This process brought three things to light – thinking outside the box to bring more value, making the right time investment, and taking calculated risks as a sales professional.

The current company I sell for offers a technology that automates labor-intensive processes in kitchens. Essentially, this eliminates risk from a manual process and makes kitchens safer. Our equipment that does the automation itself is sold on a long-term lease, so we have to sell a lot of value.

We work with all the major brands around the country, everything from the top QSR's McDonalds, Burger King, KFC, etc. to major hotels, resorts, and schools.

In 2016, we were engaged with a 20-unit Golden Corral franchisee that was one of the top franchisees in the country for the brand.

Because of the number of locations this franchisee had, we allowed the franchisee to test our program before making a long-term commitment, essentially doing a three-store pilot test so that we could collect data on the impact of our program.

We typically do this as a way for larger companies to gauge the impact and fit of our solution before they make a large-scale decision to do business with us across multiple locations.

During the test, I evaluated other ways that I could bring more value to this customer outside of what my company offered. The test was going well and I felt we would earn the long-term commitment, yet I really wanted to bring something to the table that would 100% seal the deal. This had to be something outside of what my company offered it had to pair up beautifully with our value props.

So the search began. Nearly all of us in sales have strategic partners that we lead share and network with, but how many of them can actually bring our prospects a value that aligns well with what our product or service offers? How many of them can do more than just make an introduction? How can I find a new strategic partner to deliver value that aligns with mine?

I begin spending time with some of our long-term customers and finding out the "why" behind them deciding to do business with us. I understood the core reasons, but were there other areas that the customers considered that maybe I wasn't? After making the short time investment away from prospecting to acquire a deeper understanding of why our current customers did business with us, I found a reoccurring theme through it all – safety. Almost all of our customers evaluated the safety of the kitchen before and after program implementation.

That became a sticking point for me; if I could find a strategic partner that could leverage the safety that I brought bring to the table to benefit the customer, everyone wins!

How prospects evaluate safety and injuries on the job to their staff greatly affects workers' comp rates.

I then started doing my due diligence on workers' comp insurance; all restaurant operators have to carry this to protect them from injuries that happen to their employees while on the job. When more injuries occur, their rates spike; when fewer injuries occur, their rates drop – the latter intrigued me more. If I could find an insurance company to recognize what we do to reduce injuries in kitchens, would they be more aggressive in their rates? This would be a great way to bring more value to this key franchisee while evaluating our program. This would save my prospect even more money on my program, thus, making their business more profitable. To compound it all, if this worked with this one prospect, why couldn't I scale this across nearly all of my prospects?

I began meeting with various workers comp companies and fully educating myself on everything that went into writing policies. I wanted a full understanding so that going forward, if this worked, I could talk intelligently to my prospects about the added value we now bring to the table by reducing their workers' compensation rates.

It didn't take me long to find an insurance company, do a presentation on the safety we bring to the table for restaurant owners, and put together a formalized program for my future prospects to take advantage of.

This was now a brand new, untested partnership I had with an insurance company that I was going to bring to the table during a test with one of the most well-known restaurant franchisees in the world...sounds *slightly* risky.

My new insurance partner and I put some rough numbers to paper in order to evaluate how the customer was going to look at this new offer: (I simplified these just for the book, but these were accurate high-level figures.)

Hard Costs/Savings to Prospect That I Brought to the Table

- Annual Cost of my automated program: $100,000
- Annual Hard Savings to the prospect that I bring to the table: $75,000
- *Annual Soft Savings to the prospect that I bring to the table: $45,000
- *Soft savings are those that are harder to quantify; some prospects will give you credit for these, some won't. Labor efficiency is a good example.

As you can see, we provide nice hard savings to the prospect, along with soft savings too; if combined, we are at $20k per year in savings from program implementation. However, the reality is that we do not know for sure if the prospect will give us credit for the soft savings.

Now on to what the insurance provider estimated they could do for us. This could vary because the insurance provider hadn't met with the prospect as of yet and we did not know if this would fully work.

Estimation of Annual Insurance Impact to the Prospect with the New Partnership with my Company

- Current Annual Insurance Premium - $800,000
- Estimated Adjusted Premium through the new Partnership - $750,000

I thought to myself *this is GREAT!* I now can add $50,000 to my savings per year to the prospect's bottom line. Everyone wins, the prospect gets a great deal, my new insurance agent partner picks up a new customer and I earn a new customer too. That is a true win-win-win.

However, these were all estimates on the insurance side; there was no way to be sure if it was accurate until I made the introduction and my new insurance partner could really evaluate the prospect's current business.

And to be honest, it's nearly impossible for myself, as one person, to fully screen an insurance company and their program before bringing them to the table with this operator we are in a test with. I started weighing up the risks and rewards:

Risks

- The biggest of all is whether or not I bring this insurance provider to the table and they actually increase the rates on my prospect.
- The new partner I bring to the table falls flat on execution, has poor follow-up, and doesn't provide good service – a poor reflection on myself.
- The insurance provider makes an offer to get the business and ends up cutting me out of the equation.

All are valid concerns, now here are the upsides I evaluated:

Rewards

- The insurance provider makes a great offer to the prospect and the prospect sees an incredible return for doing business with me and the insurance company.
- Everyone wins
- This works and we now have a scalable solution to bring to the table for all of our future prospects.

After thinking this through, I felt comfortable making the introduction. This was never done before in my company's history due to the risk involved, however, I felt I was doing the right thing by attempting to over-deliver to my customer.

I have always had massive success during the sales process by being as transparent as possible with prospects. So in full transparency, here is how I set up the introduction of my new insurance partner to the prospect:

"Mr. Prospect, I know you are evaluating our program for automating labor processes in your kitchen; I feel there could be some added safety benefits you may not be fully evaluating. We have a newly-formed partnership with an insurance provider that will offer a credit on your worker's comp insurance for having our automated solution in place. In full transparency, we have not tested this program with a live customer. I feel this is a good opportunity for you to see what kind of added benefit you could get from our program, and I would be open to your feedback after reviewing what my insurance partner has to offer, as this has never been done before. I want to make sure our program is the biggest success possible for you and this could be an added way for you to see that. Please let me know if you would like me to make the introduction."

That last line is important – I asked for permission to make the introduction; I've found that this is the best way to make introductions, especially if you are lead sharing. This comes off much better than just emailing a customer or prospect and CC'ing the new rep on the email. Always ask first.

It wasn't long at all before the prospect who I'd built a great relationship with accepted my offer on the introduction.

The end result through all of this exceeded my expectations. The prospect called me a few weeks later after my new partner made his proposal and told me that they will now see $150,000 savings on their premiums going into the next year because of our joint program. This well exceeded the estimated $50,000 savings the insurance rep and myself had in mind.

The prospect couldn't have been happier with me bringing them to the table and my company now has an excellent case study of added benefit to our program. They ended up signing with both of us and are seeing massive success and return on their investment.

It felt so good to hear them thank me for bringing them to the table; this really summed up consultative selling.

The lessons I learned throughout this process were big for myself as a sales professional and my company. During the time I was researching workers' comp companies, I was actually told by other reps at my company that it would not work, that it was a bad idea, and that it was too risky to bring another company to the table when I had not secured the deal myself yet. They said it would delay the sales cycle, backfire, and make myself look bad if the insurance rep didn't provide a level of service to the prospect that we would.

In the end, I went with my gut instinct. I did all the due diligence I possibly could in a short amount of time and I took a calculated risk. It was critical for me to start with my current customers and learn everything I could about their decision-making process and where they saw added benefit, rather than just going by the benefit that I saw in my own product.

Now that we have brought so much more value than we ever could as a company through an external strategic partner, we are scaling these efforts nationwide. We have an excellent case study that we are sharing with other prospects and it's growing our pipeline incrementally.

50.

WHO KNEW SELLING LOOKED LIKE THIS?

By Camille Clemons

In week 2 of my first sales job, I was asked to take on the account of a current client going through the vendor review process for a part of their operations. It was disclosed to me that there was a little "history" with the client - a few complexities, if you will. It is important to note that I'd never sold anything before in my life, at least that's what I thought. I had been with the company for a little while, but my technical sales skills were in their infancy and I knew we could not match the pricing of our competitors.

I polled the client services team and anyone who knew anything about the client, to prepare for the first meeting, where I was ready for it to be a landmine of complaints and issues. You don't know where you're going unless you know where you've been. We logged as much history as we could and once I felt sufficiently prepared (a state I would soon learn is unattainable) I scheduled the first call. It went something like this:

> Me: Hi Art, it's Camille with Vandalay Industries, it's nice to finally meet you after hearing so much about Cuyahoga Sheet Metal and your relationship with Vandalay!
> Art: Oh great, so you're my new contact, good luck!
> Me: Admittedly, I don't have all of the details, but I'm hopeful that we can talk through your experience with Vandalay

and figure out where to take it from there.

(Then I was done talking for about 30 minutes while Art gave me his story)

Finally, when he was done, I took two minutes to explain my background, experiences that would be relevant, and ask a few tough questions.

Art: It sounds like you are working to really understand our problems and help me find a solution, am I hearing you right?

Me: That's what I'm here to do. We, as a team, are committed to Cuyahoga and I am here to give you my word on that. Let's have you come to our office in Chicago to reacquaint yourself with our teams and talk through your plans for future growth.

Art: Great idea, let's get it on the calendar.

Me: After we wrap here, I'll send you a few dates that work for our team. Let's agree to have a date organized by Friday.

Art: Perfect, please copy in Rodger; he has access to the team's calendars.

A few lessons from this call have stuck with me.

- While it may be terrifying to call a not-so-happy client or prospect, if you approach it with humility and their best interests in mind, they will be grateful.

- Remind yourself that it is not about you - and never should be. Then remind yourself who pays your salary.

- Taking the time to listen and really understand a problem will best position you to come up with a creative solution. This takes time, but remember, the more time you take here, the better the relationship with your client will be – happy clients = strong business.

- You can't possibly know everything, so be okay with saying "I don't know" and be very prompt in finding someone who does.

I'm happy to report that while we didn't win that piece of business, we were given other additional work because, as a team, we took the time to understand our clients, their business, and how our solutions were relevant.

51.

DISCOVERY IS NOT JUST ONE STEP IN THE PROCESS

By Debe Rapson

During my thirty years in sales, I have honed the science and art of my discovery process to ensure that when I ask for the business, it never falls flat. Today, decisions are made through consensus and unlike the past, discovery is not done solely with one or two key stakeholders, but rather everyone on the decision team, typically between 8 to 12 people.

Coming to those discussions with a thorough understanding of the company's firmographics, both corporate initiatives and strategies will familiarize you with a high-level overview of the company's current state. Luckily, we have many easy ways to conduct such research today, and the best salespeople do their legwork before they ever reach out to ask for the meeting. Educating oneself about a prospective company prior to meeting with it is absolutely crucial to the sales process and can boost one's odds of landing a sale by leaps and bounds, as opposed to meeting with a prospect cold. I always look at a company's annual report and 10-K and spend time researching presentations on the web delivered by the key stakeholders and executives that will be making the decision. This enables me to understand their goals, challenges, ideologies, pipeline projects, etc. Furthermore, in order to figure out "who's who in the zoo," I conduct research on discover.org and LinkedIn. When I familiarize myself with a company's technology stack, I reference sites similar to builtwith.com. Other sites such as Detective by Charlie, Demandbase, and LinkedIn help me to unearth relevant topical information quickly. Lastly, before I sit down with a prospect, I follow those stakeholders on Twitter and their company on Facebook so that I can learn what they comment and care about on social media.

Today, information is easily available, so there is no reason for a salesperson not to be able to ask the probing questions that will help both the seller and prospective client. Perhaps the most important piece of advice that I can offer is not to be lazy in the preliminary stages of the sale cycle.

The job of the salesperson has changed dramatically over the past twenty years, particularly the last five, where we've seen the pace of our sales cycles slow down, a huge increase of easily accessible information and more sales processes than ever before. Salespeople are trying to figure out how to close faster, take advantage of the knowledge available, and perfect their own process down to a science. However, what remains the same is that customers buy from "genuine" people. The quickest way to earn that trusted advisor relationship is by understanding "why" they are looking to make a change, "why" they are motivated to change and "why" the company is going to fund the change.

Early in my sales career, I created my own sales process which featured the most important step: discovery. I typically would develop an in-depth list of questions, taking a personal and conversational approach. My natural curiosity and passion would always propel us three levels deeper, and this is where you uncover the reason why they have to buy. At this time, I was selling services for a high-end, high-value computer training company. Back then, computer training was a competitive industry with many low-cost providers. We couldn't compete on price, but could always win on value because of our sheer size, talent, and innovative approach. A large travel services company in my territory was looking to procure computer training for all 10,000 employees and sent out a blind request for proposal.

As part of their process, we had a short window of opportunity to question the business stakeholder (let's call her Doris); this was my opportunity, but I knew I needed to stand out from the competition. I invited Doris to our office in San Francisco, so she could see us in action. I also asked one of our lead trainers to sit in on the discussion to help me ask all the right questions; he was the expert.

We asked Doris questions focusing on training delivery, her company's experience with a provider, their need for additional support, and why. We wanted to understand what the company was looking to accomplish with this investment and what failure and success would subsequently look like. We inquired how she got to be the project lead and what would make her look good to the executives. Her answers got us excited about this project and she could see that we were genuinely interested in helping them transform the skill set of their workforce. Our lead trainer suggested additional criteria that would make their project more successful and ensure that the computer training skills would stick. Our sixty-minute session grew into two hours as we asked deeper questions that morphed into a plan that would quickly add long-term value for their teams.

That discussion was the catalyst for a long-term relationship that began with creating a champion and establishing the framework for partnership with Doris.

We continued to align the things we learned that day with our differentiators. After we were awarded a multi-million dollar contract, Doris later told me that they felt heard that first day we met and we gave them confidence that we would deliver their desired outcome.

One can't solve problems without understanding "the why." At this point in my career, I hadn't yet developed my process, but it became clear to me that I stumbled upon a formula during this meeting that would forever change my approach to discovery.

Lessons Learned:

A well thought out discovery process does the following things for you:

- Determines whether an account is your ideal customer or is simply going to be a waste of your precious time and energy.

- Captures your customer's true needs and their definition of value to precisely match your solution to what they ideally would like to buy.

- Uncovers a prospect's complete decision-making process right from the start, allowing you to know exactly what you need to do each step of the way in order to win their business.

A well-thought-out discovery process does the following things for your prospect:

- Establishes a partnership approach.

- Helps them to uncover what they haven't thought about or didn't know.

- Establishes your credibility.

While conducting discovery....

- Be warm – develop rapport through common connections, interests & backgrounds.

- Be genuinely curious... People know when you are faking it.

- Establish credibility through storytelling – Know your facts.

- Gaint trust through listening and not selling.

- Be honest... If you can't solve their problem, tell then and make a suggestion.

Tips/Tricks for discovery:

- Enter every meeting prepared with everything you could find about the company.

- Take Great Notes/NOT on your computer-it's distracting and loud.

- Triangulate it with other key stakeholders.

- Deliver highly-personalized presentations with what you learned.

- Remind prospects of the value to them via objection handling.

- Hold them accountable to what they shared.

What if you could create so much value in your customer's mind that they would want your solution no matter what the price? This is how you do get it done....

Debe Rapson's Bio 13
11. Courage Drives Positive Outcomes 63

52.

DEAL QUALIFICATION. HOW I USED TO LOSE ~40% OF MY DEALS TO A SINGLE COMPETITOR

By Jelle den Dunnen

How much impact can 2 questions really have on your sales success? If I hadn't experienced the impact myself, I would have answered that the impact would be hardly visible, a maximum of 10% or so, but no more than that, right?

Taking a step back, why did I lose 40% of my deals to a single competitor? Looking back, I would say it was down to stubbornness and eagerness.

Being in sales, we sometimes (most times) suffer from the conviction that we are invincible. While my other story is focused on mindset, I did raise a point on being realistic as well. Sometimes we just need to wake up and realize that we can't win every deal.

Some might say that there can only be one winner in a deal. Think again; there are more! If we're not talking about the person that walks away with a bottle of champagne, oh, sorry, I mean signature, who are we then talking about? Who else could be winning in the pursuit?

When I was first asked the question, I didn't know the answer, but it makes so much sense.

The other person that wins in a deal is the one that gets out of the cycle early.

Have you quantified how much time you spend on deals that you were never going to win in the first place? Probably not. You probably don't want to hear the answer to the question! I sure didn't.

This brings me to the other reason why I lost that much to a competitor, eagerness. If we can get into a cycle, we just want to participate. Why would we turn it down?

Is it because I'm too busy? Nah, of course not. Bring it on, I can handle one more!

Is it because the requirements are out of whack? Nope, I'll re-engineer the vision!

Perhaps it is because we're column fodder and the competition is way ahead of us? I'll give it a try and see if I can turn it around!

These are just a few of the excuses we give ourselves to ignore the fact that we can't turn a deal down without having a go at it. Right?

Like I said, our eagerness to get into another sales cycle and our stubbornness of not being able to walk away is causing us to waste a lot of time on deals that we were never going to win in the first place.

I love data and enjoy analyzing it, maybe a little bit too much sometimes, but as such, I was reviewing the deals that I had been working on all year and looked at the reasons I lost, as well as which competitor I lost to.

That's when I realized that I was losing ~40% of my deals to a single competitor. That's HUGE right, and after further analysis, losing 40% of my deals to this fierce competitor wasn't due to the strengths of that competition; it was because I was too stubborn to walk away and too convinced that my existing sales strategies would work. Essentially, I was too eager to get into those sales cycles.

I was so surprised to find out that I lost more opportunities due to the fact that the 'buyer' didn't purchase anything at all than I lost to an actual competitor. Yes, you're reading it right; the most frequent value in the 'lost to' field in my CRM was No Change At All. While the reasons why I lost them had some variables, it all came down to the prospect either not feeling the need to change or not seeing the value of changing towards our product/service, or that of our real competitors.

I must admit, I didn't know how to handle or change that directly, so I discussed it with my peers. I don't remember how we eventually got there, but suddenly we realized it was not the prospect who was to blame here for wasting our time - we were to blame! We found out that I wasn't the only one with that experience.

The stubbornness and eagerness prevented us from recognizing why these prospects were likely not to buy anything. So, the only one that could make a change to that, would be me. Therefore, I started reviewing these deals in more detail and, eventually, I recognized certain trends and approaches.

Sometimes prospects told me what I wanted to hear, a dangerous thing, of which I'm sure we have all experienced, and it's tough to call that out. However, what I realized was that while I was asking questions in the right direction, but not asking the right questions to flush these people out that weren't going to buy. I knew their challenges and they told me their requirements, as well as somewhat of a buying process. Although several of them gave me true buying signals, it just wasn't enough. They often were looking to improve their existing environment, but they couldn't quantify the challenges with the status quo. I mean, it's very easy to fall for the comment: "If what you have to offer is better than what we have today and will improve our situation, we will buy it." At first, it sounds marvelous, but define better and define improvement - how can you measure that? If you can't measure it, you can't recognize the difference, meaning the prospect won't be able to put a numerical value on it.

The above makes sense; however, that's where stubbornness tricks us again. It's not the prospect's responsibility to put a recognizable value to something; it's our responsibility. It's our job to make the prospect aware of that value and get them to agree to it.

Haha, I made some mistakes with that last one as well - revealing the value to a prospect, thinking they got it, and just moving on. Long story short, just make sure you confirm that the prospect really understands the necessary information before doing anything else.

So how did I change it? As mentioned before, I wasn't asking the right questions, or better said, I wasn't asking the questions in the right way. There were 2 questions that I surely hadn't thought of myself, but I took these two questions and made them an entire topic of their own in a prospect pursuit.

Oh, and they are so simple. **Why are we here?** And **what happens if you don't buy?**

Of course, I had asked these questions many times before, but like with selling certain features, products or impacts, you need to build it up, put weight behind it, and make it very important.

I can remember a certain deal in Belgium where I asked these questions, looked at them straight on, and remained silent. A few seconds went by, and another few seconds, yup, almost getting awkward here… haha, but then it happened. The stakeholders turned to each other and started debating amongst themselves, trying to answer these questions. I just sat there watching, listening, and doing nothing. It was amazing… like Julius Caesar said; "Veni, vidi, vici."

After about 10-15 minutes of debate (where they clearly had different positions), they had called out their key pains and articulated their business goals, but also quantified the impact of what would happen if they didn't make a change. Due to those 2 questions, they realized that if they didn't make any change, they would fail to achieve their business goals on time, and hence they had to make a change. Essentially, they were finally able to consciously, and in a very clear manner, tell me why we were there.

It was smooth sailing from there on out, and they signed about 8 weeks later.

This is a perfect example of how these questions impacted my success, and I would rather say "topics" because many questions relate to these 2 important ones. However, it has been an amazing experience, trying to perfect the conversations we are having around these 2 topics and I couldn't be more thankful to my peers who helped me along the way.

So what happened to that 40%?

While I still lose to no change, it has drastically decreased. This is due to many different factors, some of which I have no control of. Last year, I managed to get to an 82% win rate on qualified deals. That would have absolutely been lower if it wasn't for these 2 questions, don't you think?

53.

THE YEAR I DOUBLED MY INCOME

By David Weiss

Imagine for a second you are, at least in your mind, the best at something, and up to this point in your life, mostly, you have been proven correct. That was me, basking in my glorious ignorance. I had done some amazing things and had been living a sales career I was proud of. I had made consistent multiple six figure incomes, hit or exceeded plan every year at every company I had been part of, won multiple Presidents' Clubs to some of the best destinations in the world. I've hired and trained people who have hit their goals, and taken on initiatives that have helped to shape the strategy and culture of multiple organizations. I thought I was elite. I thought I had this sales thing figured out. Boy was I wrong.

At this point in my career, it was rare for me to get pushed, and pushed hard, on my sales ability. After all, I was successful, and working in a senior level sales role at a Fortune 250 company. I've read many books on sales, and as I mentioned in my other story, been trained by some great people and companies. After Aramark, I went on to Career-Builder, which has been consistently ranked as one of the best companies to sell for, with the best training, as has the Fortune 250 company I was working for at the time. However, along came a leader who flipped my world upside down. When Gregory Donovan was first assigned to my team, I took the approach of, "Who is this new guy and what can he do for me?" (As I get older, wiser and frankly realize how stupid I am, I have learned that it's important to allow people to challenge me, and this person did like no other). He had been a successful enterprise salesperson for years, started his own company and sold it, and was well connected with heads of sales at some huge companies. He quickly showed me I had much more room to grow.

Let me be humbly honest; there are times in sales or in anything, where you experience much success and you get complacent. You expect that your success will keep going, because why wouldn't it? You forget that to get where you have gotten, you had to earn it, DAILY. Not only did Gregory smack that reality back into me, but he also showed me how much more I could be doing, and in turn, how much more I could be making. He quickly, and in a rather stoic way, showed me he was the master and I was the student; he painted a new reality for me I had to achieve.

Ok, so how did he shake my foundation? Oddly enough, it was easier than I thought possible; he simply asked me during one of our goal setting meetings, "How much money do you want to make this fiscal?" I told him what I thought was a solid number. He laughed in a very encouraging way and said, "You're better than that." I challenged him because I thought the number I had given him was a good number. I remember this moment because a weird emotion hit me when he told me I could do more. It was part anger ("How dare you question me? I already do so much; what can doing more really achieve?" – law of diminishing returns). There was also some fear in there (around maybe I am not as good as I think I am). Honestly, I didn't believe him. I didn't know how to do more than I was or see how doing more would even translate into more. With a very simple question, he shined a light on a blind spot.

What followed was almost a discovery session, similar to what we all put our clients through. Again, we were new to our relationship together, so he sought to understand everything I was doing (he already had some idea) and to get me to explain my process. He learned everything about how I worked and what I did. At the end, as if he already knew the answer, he said, you are good, but you can do more. I simply said, "How?"

Let's take a quick pause here.

I am going to leave you with some important things in this paragraph, and I will get into exactly how to make changes that will forever impact you. More important, you must be coachable. I am not the only person he asked this information from and gave this information to, but I am the one who took the coaching and ran with it. I have always believed that if you want to be the best, you need to be open to learning. You need to be humble, to seek people better than you and to be open to getting a punch of reality. I would argue that the most important thing a salesperson needs to be in their career is coachable.

Ok, let's resume, "How would I double my income?" He told me some obvious stuff. It was clear I needed to prospect more, so he challenged me to figure it out. I needed to up my game by building better business cases, and push executives for data, alignment, validation, and change. This would lead to deeper discovery sessions--discovery that takes twice as long as the presentation to follow. However, most important, he would teach me a new methodology that changed my game forever.

This was called MEDDPICC.

So what do these 8 letters that will forever change your life in sales mean?

METRICS – What is the business case? Think of the hard dollars, real value, and improvements in KPIs that your solution brings that justify a change. This is an actual mathematical equation, not a guess.

ECONOMIC BUYER – Who can spend money, has budget, can CREATE budget, and can sign a contract?

DECISION CRITERIA – What is their wish list? What items will you be measured on and need to achieve to earn their business?

DECISION PROCESS – Who is involved? When do they want to make a decision? When do they want to go live?

PAPER PROCESS – What is the legal process a company will go through? Who are the people involved? How long does it take them to review, redline, and give approval for signature? This is critical to learning to make sure deals close on time.

IDENTIFY PAIN – What are the real issues, goals, and outcomes? This, along with metrics, helps solidify the "Why Change" message.

CHAMPIONS – Who will give you inside information and sell for you when you are not there?

COMPETITION – Who are they? What differentiates you from them? What landmines can you set?

The above criteria are color coded, red, yellow, or green. Your job during the sales process is to get them all to green as fast as possible. Red is information you don't know. Yellow is information you know some of, but it may not be 100% validated. Green means you are 100% confident it is complete and validated by the client.

Now you may be saying to yourself, "David, this stuff is obvious." Yes, yes it is. It was to me when I first saw it, too. However, I went back and applied it to the deals I was working, the ones I had lost, and the ones I had won. Let's just say, my mind was blown. Out of over 50 opportunities across a 20 million dollar pipeline, I didn't win a single deal that still had MEDDPICC criteria still in the red, and all the deals I won had all the criteria in green. Had I known this before, I would have won much more business. Now I challenge you, as I was challenged, pick a deal you are working. Write out the eight letters and be honest with filling in the information. I bet you anything that you have red and yellow all over it. How much is really green?

I will pause here.

Seriously, go do this….I'm waiting…

Now, go do it on the last deal you lost…

Now, go do it on the last deal you won…

You're welcome!

Again, we are all at different stages of our sales development, but this here will change your life. It will show you your blind spots, help you prepare for meetings, and WILL help you win more. It is a race to get these into green faster than your competition. Whoever gets all this information the fastest, and in a complete fashion, will often win. Now, nothing is guaranteed in this world; you could do everything right and still lose. However, using this methodology will increase your chance of winning dramatically.

To wrap this up, seek people who can make you better. (Shout out to Gregory Donovan again here, thanks for everything, Greg! You forever changed my life.) Be coachable, don't be lazy, AND use MEDDPICC.

54.

WELL THAT SUCKED

By Camille Clemons

Let's set the stage:

- New prospect.

- Well-known firm.

- Looking for a long-term partner to support their growth plans.

- Team members from three offices flying in...

You've heard it before, but it's nonetheless worth mentioning here: there is absolutely no replacement for preparation.

This wasn't any ordinary Tuesday; this Tuesday we were in the big leagues, pitching our core business to a huge prospect. We had a few internal conference calls to prepare an agenda, discuss handoffs throughout, outline the system demo, etc. The meetings were short and, looking back, maybe a little dismissive. "Yeah we've got this, we've done it together a hundred times. Safe travels and see you Tuesday."

We met outside their building on Park Avenue looking like a well-oiled machine with shined shoes and bright eyes. After check in at the lobby desk, we took the elevator up to the floor, one from the top. While the IT expert helped us connect to the Wi-Fi network, I put an agenda and a nicely branded keepsake at each seat, and then we waited. After a few minutes, their team walked in and the lug bolts on the wheels began to loosen.

One by one, we shook hands, and then we shook more hands. Pretty soon, the room was at its capacity and there was no more room for anyone to sit down. However, they kept coming. Maybe they didn't expect us to have four people? Maybe they heard we were coming and word spread how dynamic our solution was and everyone wanted to hear the presentation? Maybe the decision was being made by committee? As it turns out, seating would end up being the least of our problems and the car got a little wobbly.

To this point, SRO (Standing Room Only) for a finals presentation sounds like a dream. We begin. I introduce myself and the balance of the room gives their intros. I go over the agenda and we start the presentation. As I mentioned, we knew how they ran their business, what was important to them, and what we needed in order to impress the room. After highlighting stats about our business, the lead on their side asked how many clients with investment strategies like theirs we serviced today. Pretty standard question. Crickets. After a period of uncomfortable silence, we came up with a less-than-relevant statistic to cite, which was at least better than nothing. Then we moved to the demo portion of the day. The system was down, not the Wi-Fi, but our main delivery system. However, it was not just down, it was down for maintenance. Probably should have checked that...

There are fifty more samples of what-not-to-dos I could pull from that afternoon, but as the lug nuts flew off each wheel one by one, there was nothing I could do. Maybe I didn't have enough years of experience to redeem the day or I didn't understand exactly what they wanted. No excuses - I just didn't prepare. Checking boxes and having canned statistics may be enough to make it through some presentations, but not this one, and I should have done more. I probably rested a little too hard on my laurels and our combined team experience in presentation, but not enough on what I felt deep-down what I needed to do. From that day on, I've made sure to continually remind myself that how I do anything is how I do everything.

55.

TAKE TIME FOR RESEARCH AND ALWAYS DO A DRY RUN

By Trey Simonton

Ever since I started my career, sales leadership has harped on about how important it is to research and be knowledgeable about a company before you speak to a prospect. I have heard, internalized and now believe that people buy from people they trust. This is true in enterprise software; sales buyers look to salespeople to be advisors. They want to ensure that you know their business, understand their goals and can limit their risk to ensure a successful solution deployment.

As I stated, I have heard and internalized the importance of strong research and preparation before a meeting, but several times throughout my career, my laziness and lack of preparation punched me in the mouth.

HIPPA vs. HIPAA

The first occurred about 15 years ago on a trip to Chicago to meet with a health insurance provider. To this point in my career, I had developed a fair amount of expertise selling to both retailers and financial institutions like banks and brokers. I was selling a data integration software platform at the time and was excited about the upcoming meeting. Two days before the meeting, I learned about the Health Insurance Portability and Accountability Act (HIPAA) that would make management and compliance of the insurance company's data crucially important. Without doing much research, I quickly wove HIPPA (*not HIPAA*) into the cover slide of my presentation to demonstrate how our software could help them with compliance challenges.

Increase your Focus on Data Quality to Ensure HIPPA Compliance

Data quality was of tremendous interest to everyone in the company's IT and compliance departments, so both the Chief Information Officer (CIO) and the Chief Compliance Officer (CCO) were scheduled to attend. In response, I ensured that my sales engineer, my Division Vice President and the head of our Healthcare practice would be in attendance. Unfortunately, everyone from our team was arriving in Chicago just before the meeting, and we could not review the overview presentation as a team.

We opened the meeting at the insurance company's office with a round of introductions to over a dozen total attendees from the insurance company's IT and compliance departments. Shortly after I projected my opening slide, the conversation came to a complete halt. Although I was unaware of my error, the acronym HIPPA (*not HIPAA*) stood out at the center of the opening slide. The Chief Compliance Officer spoke up sharply, stating, "Trey, while I appreciate the effort for you and your team to travel across the country to meet with us here in Chicago, we will have to end this meeting at this time. It is clear to me that you know <u>nothing</u> about our challenges with the new HIPAA compliance issues and I see no reason to move forward."

Wow! I was crushed! I sat and watched as every participant from the insurance company got up and left the room one-by-one. I was left with my sales engineer, Division Vice President and the head of our

Healthcare practice looking at me, blown away by my mistake. It was an extremely costly error and one I vowed never to repeat. Sometimes, we can get in too big of a hurry to say something inspirational or make an impact with our presentation.

Looking back, there are so many things I could have done differently. I could have done more research, ensured I was prepared a few days earlier and, of course, shared the presentation for the team to review, or even scheduled time to review and rehearse as a team before the meeting. I still remember my Division Vice President sending me a copy of all the expense reports submitted by the team to show me how much my oversight had cost the company. The simple message from my DVP was, "Don't let it happen again!"

Hot Water Heater vs. Water Heater

The "HIPPA" mishap stuck with me for a long time and changed the way I researched and prepared for meetings. Fast forward about ten years, and I started a new position with a large Ratings & Reviews company selling enterprise software to capture the Voice of the Customer. I had been asked to call on a large manufacturer of water heaters whom I knew was spending aggressively that year on new marketing and branding initiatives.

Before an upcoming onsite meeting with the Chief Marketing Officer (CMO) and his staff, I hosted multiple prep sessions with my sales engineer and my team's Vice President of Sales. We could get consumers and plumbers talking with ratings & reviews about what made this manufacturer's water heaters better than the competition and help drive more sales for the company both online and in-store.

The night before the meeting, we hosted the CMO and his staff for dinner and had a great discussion. In the weeks leading to the meeting, I developed a great coach on the CMO's staff and had received lots of feedback on what the CMO would want to see in the presentation. As we started the meeting, I had my opening slide projected on the screen to set the tone for the session. The CMO sat down, looked up, paused for effect with frustration on his face and stated, "Trey, there is no such thing as a *cold-water heater*. Why do you feel the need to state *hot water heater* in your slides? *It is simply a water heater!*" The CMO went on, "I am going to get up and leave the room and grab a cup of coffee. By the time I return, you need to find and remove every mention of the phrase *hot water heater* in your presentation."

I had flashbacks to the "HIPAA" fiasco and didn't want to repeat that same experience. The rest of the session, our entire team spoke and presented on pins and needles, careful not to say the phrase "*hot water heater.*" It was harder than you might think because we, as consumers, say it all the time - *hot water heater*. Two months later, we agreed to terms and finalized a partnership with the CMO. We listened, understood why something as basic as the term "*water heater*" was a priority to him, and made that one pillar of our program as we amplified the voice of the customer.

**Get Consumers and Plumbers talking about
why they love your Hot Water Heaters**

Whenever you make mistakes, it is always important to look back and determine what you can improve on to avoid repeating those same slip-ups. I mentioned before that I developed a great coach in the account. In the weeks before the meeting, I could have easily shared a copy of the presentation ensuring our message would resonate. But, I missed my opportunity then. Now I try to engage my coaches early as part of the sales process and ask for their buy-in as I prepare materials to turn them into a champion.

56.

UNDERSTANDING AN OPPORTUNITY'S TRUE VALUE

By George Penyak

You always hear in sales the tale that is as old as time – you need to network. You need to have a network, grow it, manage it, leverage it and keep it top-of-mind.

For many sales newbies (and unfortunately some sales veterans), this sounds exhausting. I've heard reps in the past say, "I am only going to focus my networking efforts with my key accounts and customers" or "My time is too valuable to spend networking with smaller accounts."

This is a very short-sighted approach to growing your business and clientele. I know that at face value it seems counterintuitive to spend much time networking with your current customers; most of us that are in true hunter roles are focused on new accounts obtained, since that is where real incremental dollars are made for you and your company.

Since that is the case, doesn't it make sense to focus all of your networking efforts on your larger opportunities and customers? Not necessarily now, of course, but you need to spend your time wisely; there is some wisdom in balancing your networking efforts with the size of the opportunity. Networking often holds the keys to the castle of obtaining larger accounts, but you have to understand the power that one decision maker could have at a smaller-to-medium-size opportunity. As a result, it's very wise to not judge an opportunity from the outside looking in.

You shouldn't always invest your time in direct correlation with opportunity size.

Remember, you don't know what you don't know – judging each of your opportunities by size is just one simple way to evaluate where to spend your time. A better way to organize your opportunities is by impact. By impact, I am referring to what I call the "ripple effect" that one account could have on your book of business and company.

What if you were researching two different opportunities in your portfolio (one very small and one very large) and you found out that the owner of the smaller deal was close friends with the owner of the larger deal? Would that smaller opportunity start to get more of your attention? Of course it would!

If you can map out who knows who in your marketplace, then you can strategically arrange a roadmap to dominate your marketplace. In my business, it greatly shortens the sales cycle when you can leverage a relationship with a current customer.

You may find a path to a large account by working a smaller account with a shorter sales cycle, with the end goal of getting an introduction to that larger account by way of your new customer.

Wouldn't those small deals get way more important to you if you knew exactly who that decision maker knows in the marketplace?

When evaluating your opportunities, do some relationship mapping at a 30,000-foot level. Map out your opportunities and decision makers, finding connections. That is where you can piece together the fastest road to success.

Then you can start to sort your opportunities by impact, think like this - where can one new account gained lead me without having to start from scratch on another account?

There are a few different methods you can use to build out a relationship map for your opportunities.

LinkedIn – search for your targets' connections, past employment, the charities they support, the colleges they attended, etc.

Committees and Boards (searching online) – many key decision makers and CEOs sit on various boards with other professionals in similar roles.

Working backward – network with the customers you already have and/or those that have bought from you in the past. This is a great place to start.

Ground-up approach – when you build out internal coaches within a target company, specifically look for longer-tenured employees to focus on. Ask good questions to learn about the decision maker and who they might know.

I've benefited a lot from accounts where other competitive reps didn't spend the time with the decision maker. They didn't take the time to fully understand the span of the impact that the one decision maker could have outside of his/her organization. They looked at the account from the outside looking in and saw that the account was only a fraction of the size of other accounts that they needed to sell, so they gave a minimal effort towards it.

You can't judge an account by the size of its business, sales revenue, number of employees, etc. The best way to have long-term sustainable success in sales is to look at it as a people business, not a numbers business. If it was that easy, everyone would be a top 1% producer by playing the sales funnel game and pumping as much as you can in your sales funnel – in other words, we'd have a lot of "top producers" out there.

If you own a territory, I believe you can play the sales funnel game and be a top producer, but in the long run, you will end up spending less time on each opportunity – because you're looking for a quick "yes" or "no" and then moving on. I just do not feel that is fully sustainable for long-term success. You're really passing up on the true gold that could lie within a particular account – understanding who that decision-maker knows. The great salespeople out there can see value beyond the account; they can visualize what an account would mean to their company and book of business regardless of the size of the account itself.

One of the best years I have had so far in my sales career, I finished number one in my company with 235% to the goal at year's end and no, I did not sell one massive account to boost my number ahead of my fellow reps. I worked a large number of small-to-medium-sized accounts, but I worked them in the most efficient way possible – through the decision maker's network.

Take a look at the example below:

What the sales funnel rep sees:

    Company A – 35 locations
    Company B – 15 locations
    Company C – 2 locations
    Company D – 1 locations
    Company E – 75 locations
    Company F – 7 locations
    Company G – 60 locations
    Company H – 100 locations
    Company I – 200 locations

Just the numbers right?

Most hunters would skim over the small and medium-sized opportunities and go right after the whales, Companies E, G, H, & I.

A rep could 3x their annual number with one sale – jackpot, right?! Well maybe, but let's peel back a layer and look at their opportunities holistically:

Company A – 35 locations – Company A's CEO is based in Charleston, SC, and has owned these locations for 30 years. He sits on the statewide association board.

Company B – 15 locations – Company B's CEO is currently the statewide association chairman for the board for this sector.

Company C – 2 locations – Company C's CEO is the president of the local association's chapter and is also based in Charleston SC.

Company D – 1 location – This CEO got his start by previously working for Company B's current CEO.

Company E – 75 locations – This CEO grew up as best

friends with company B's CEO.

Company F – 7 locations – Company F's CEO played in a charity golf tournament with Company A's CEO – also based in Charleston, SC.

Company G – 60 locations - Company G has a new CEO from outside the local territory.

Company H – 100 locations – Company H's owner is based in the market but has little to do with associations or boards.

Company I – 200 locations – Company I's CEO spends little time in the market and travels often.

It almost now looks like a puzzle, but if you look closely, you can see good connections between many smaller/medium-sized opportunities. The saying that everybody knows somebody is true, and is very true in business. I am sure the CEOs of Company H and I have a good network; that network just happens to be outside of my market - not that it's a bad thing, it just makes them less accessible to me. If they are less accessible to me, it tells me that there is a long road ahead of me in the sales process. So I adjusted where I was going to spend my time.

Now, let's back up – how did I get this information? CEOs don't just take every phone call and share who they know with everyone. I got this info by often working from the ground up on each account. I spent time meeting with lower-level employees that have been employed at that company for a long time. Good CEOs typically know long-time employees by name due to their loyalty, and those are good places to start. Sometimes you get the best information on an account from lower-level managers and employees. They often know details about the CEO and the company itself that the CEO would not be willing to share with you.

An added plus to doing research with long-time employees is that when you get to the CEO's table, you can name drop those long-time employees you spent time with. Most of the time, they will appreciate that and you will feel closer to them because you know their culture and people.

You can also use the online methods I laid out earlier in this chapter to get much of this information.

Now with all that being said, it's much easier and quicker to get access to the CEO of a one location company vs. a company that operates at the scale of 20-100x that.

Once I found out from a long-time employee at company D (1 location) that the CEO got his start from working with company B's CEO, I knew I was on to something. I could get a quick close on this single location company but, more importantly, gain a good connection to the 15-unit CEO at Company B. If company B's CEO is the chairman of the statewide board, well now we're cooking with gas!

It didn't take long to close company D and build a big advocate in that company's CEO. I strategically put a lot of resources and time into closing that one small deal and building a great relationship with the single unit CEO at company B.

Long story short, I was able to penetrate the marketplace through introductions from CEO to CEO. I closed the following accounts all by starting with the smallest account in my portfolio:

> **Company D – 1 location** – This was the first deal of the string that I closed.
>
> **Company B – 15 locations** – Company D lead me to this introduction and deal. Once I added this CEO to my network things really started to come together in my market.
>
> **Company A – 35 locations** – Company B and A were so closely related that both of these deals closed at nearly the same time.
>
> **Company C – 2 locations** – Closing company A made this deal very smooth and quick, people talk and idea share even at the CEO level.
>
> **Company E – 75 locations** – This was the biggest deal of them all. This deal would not have happened had I not closed company B first.
>
> **Company F – 7 locations** – This was the final deal that I closed.

In summary, this is more about just doing your research on your market; it's a little deeper than that. It's about finding personal connections within your market and understanding who knows who, as well as how they know each other. Once you've built this out, leverage it and find the path of least resistance, I would much rather close a small deal that I know could open a door to a larger deal down the road, than spend time calling on the larger deal cold. Don't overcomplicate it; sales is a people and relationship game. Happy hunting!

57.

THE FOUR "FS" TO BUILDING THE RIGHT MOMENTUM WITH CUSTOMERS

By Phil Terrill

Over the past couple of years, being able to observe and sell within the Microsoft ecosystem to our customers, I learned that they have a ton of complex problems. They demand everything from us and require a "white glove" experience at all times. I'm sure you are wondering what this has to do with the Four "Fs" to help build the right momentum with customers. Well, the model actually helped me hit my quota while doing right by my customers. These will help you really compartmentalize your efforts with customers or partners:

#1 - Find what your customers are trying to accomplish and go deep into that problem statement. Once you identify the one or two major areas, you can ask logical questions to help build solutions that work for your customer! The outcome is typically very insightful and rewarding, in that you create a champion with your customer. Take the time to do the dirty work and get in the trenches. The more you understand their goals, the better you can align solutions, experts, and partners. People like doing business with those who understand the business, see the vision, and are willing to do whatever it ethically takes to get the job done. (That might even mean being creative to stay at or under budget, but I will leave that up to you!) Doing things in good spirit creates incredible "sales karma" that any business person can appreciate on any day!

#2 - Focus on what makes you, YOU! Everyone has incredible talents and a unique set of skills that position them to be at this shared destination in front of customers. My thinking two and half years ago was that I was not a "technical" guy, but I loved technology. I grew up with technology and embraced the monumental impact it had on influencing 21st-century commerce. Now, why would your customers care about your "incredible talents and unique set of skills" when discussing business? In the simplest form, customers are just people at the end of the day. As a result, the more we can personalize our engagements and remove the ambition to make another sale (or retire quota), the more business gets accomplished. Transformational solutions lead to bigger deals and your passion to innovate drives the customer to invest in new areas of their business. Focus on you!

#3 - Feed yourself with both qualitative (non-technical) and quantitative (technical) knowledge about your own solution/product stack. The better you can tell stories that connect to tangible results, the easier your life will be as an extension of your customer. Once your customer can feel like you have the expertise to deliver, you will receive the elusive "green light," meaning it's full speed ahead to knock the project out of the park. This moment is a continuous process, because the great business folks I have met "knowledge- share" with their customers. This exchange of information leads to accountability in both directions, ensuring that learning is a priority. Decisions are made with the right information at the right time! It sounds simple, but you have to make time to learn and pass it forward.

#4 - Facts are the bloodline to winning your customers' trust! Emphasize the value to their business and establish a partnership as your priority. Think about your own relationships - fluff and lies do not usually result in positive relationships. Communicating the "data truth" about product capabilities, roadmaps, enhancements, gaps, etc. will be the key to expanding your ability to land broader investments from your customer. They see the same picture you do. That is customer obsession through transparency!

All in all, these four gems, or "Fs" will help you to keep pushing the needle and accomplishing the unmentioned "F" - Finish! None of these matter if you do not finish or do right by your customers. In my last story, I wanted to share an experience that helped turn a dormant customer into a full-on evangelist.

58.

OVERCOMING THE PRICE OBJECTION

By AJ Brasel

It doesn't matter what product or service is being sold, the price is always the most common objection for all sales professionals. At some point in everyone's sales career, there will be a desire to lower a price point to razor-thin margins in order to get a deal done. So many prospective customers will attempt to drive down the cost of a product or service and push back on a rep to get "the best deal." The easy way out is to give in, get the quick sale, and move on to the next prospect. While taking the easy way out is obviously very appealing and the fastest way to get the commission – lowering your price is a horrible tactic for long-term success. The low-price tactic devalues your product and gives the customer all the control. The next sales rep to walk into their door with a product that is a penny lower is going to steal that business. By selling on the price, you are essentially removing all the value from the sale and, if you don't lose that business on price, down the line you can rest assured that your customer will come back for reductions in the future. The only way to overcome the pricing objection is to add value to the sale that cannot be measured financially. By doing this, the price objection becomes null and void. Your customer will thus not be able to compare you to a price-driven sales rep in the future because you are bringing additional value to the business. This keeps the control in your hands and gives you the opportunity to cultivate a long-lasting, mutually-beneficial relationship. How do you add value? It is obviously going to be determined by what you sell and who you sell to. In my personal experience, I sell through the channel, meaning my customers resell my product. I'll outline my tactics below...

Have a full understanding of your customer's business

Whenever I take over an account or win a new business, I make sure that I identify all the key decision-makers throughout the organization. Typically, it takes more than one individual to decide on which vendor to do business with. I make sure that I have a very detailed conversation with each of those individuals to discover what their job entails and what value I can bring to their daily activities. I only pitch solutions that would directly impact that individual. Once the business has been on-boarded, I continue to work my way through the business and create relationships with any individual that interacts with my company. The goal is to be a reliable point of contact for all individuals in that organization, so whenever they look at other options, the prospect of change creates pain throughout the company. All of my customers are extremely different in their background, focus, and approach. I take time to fully understand the sales strategy of the organization, which includes how they go to market, what their annual goals are, and how they compensate their sales team. From there, I can advise my customer on what I've seen from other similar organizations that have had success. I bring an outsider's insight into their business and add value through being an advisor. Whenever my company brings new products or services to market, I know which of my customers these would apply to and who to approach in those organizations to sell them to. Having this full understanding allows me to be efficient and concise in my sales approach.

Work Directly with the Sales Team

The customers I work with that have a sales team have typically been trained on my offering. Most of them have so many different products, they focus on making sure I stay in front of them; winning their mindshare is extremely important. I have worked with most of the sales reps individually on different opportunities that have required some creativity on my company's part in order to win. Whenever some of those reps have complex opportunities, they typically call me to sort through the nuances and plug in where necessary. The sales team typically sees me as a resource to help them in their success and the leadership team sees me as an asset because I am helping to drive profitability into their organization.

Add Only Services that Fit that Organization

This goes hand in hand with my first point. So many sales reps try to throw as much at their accounts as possible and hope that something sticks. Whenever I have that full understanding of the customer's organization, I know what services fit that specific organization. I can fully pitch my services to the right people within their company and help them implement efficiently. This allows me to add a massive amount of value-added services on top of my product throughout an account that ties me in as the vendor. The services that my company adds create efficiency and enhance profitability in that organization. Additionally, I have introduced different subject matter experts to the account and created bonds with my company that extend beyond me.

Once I'm fully embedded within that organization and have a few services added into the company, price no longer becomes a concern with the buying team. This is because the process of another company coming in and starting fresh becomes very painful at that point. My close relationship allows customers to share challenges and areas for improvement more openly with me, which allows me to tackle their issues quickly and efficiently. I have added services throughout the organization that are tied to my company and have embedded myself into their infrastructure. My top customers look to me and my company to help them formulate their annual goals and strategy. The value of the services provided to their organizations outweighs the lower pricing that someone else can offer them.

59.

LET ME KNOW IF ANYTHING CHANGES

By DeJuan Brown

Losing a sale can be devastating, no matter the size of the deal.

I mean the time, effort, and energy we expend to get to the finish line is real.

To get all the way there and not get the deal across impacts so many areas of our lives.

I believe there is a specific type of fatigue that stems from hearing 'thanks for all your time, but we've decided to go another route.'

Several years into my career, my final responses to this rebuff were almost always identical.

I'd often ask the normal, "What made you decide to go that route?" and then finally I'd muster up the strength to utter the dreaded 8-word cliché:

"No problem, **let me know if anything changes.**"

In 5+ years, amazingly, nothing ever changed! At least, not enough changed to prompt a prospect to call me back.

Honestly, I never thought twice about whether my statement would ever even garner a future response.

I was on auto-response when the deal was lost, and being that disconnected from the prospect at the end probably meant that I was disconnected from the beginning.

It wasn't until I started hearing talk about concepts like servant-leadership, service first and customer-centrism that I had an epiphany of some sort.

Well, it was not the kind of epiphany that leads to wholesale change. However, I had enough interest to try some short-term experimentation with these concepts.

The first thing I tried ended up being a game-changer, and I can point to at least three consistent results which persist to this day.

Instead of the dismissive and uncaring "let me know if anything changes," I shifted my focus to what I term the "continuity of service."

I would make helping my prospect my primary goal in my sales meetings. I know many of you are thinking, "DUH!!! What other goals would you have?"

If I'm honest, I had a ton of goals in my meetings during that time. However, at least 90% were singular and self-serving. I wanted the prospect to know all the things my solution could do for them, how long we'd taken to develop these unique features, what other clients were saying about our solution, etc.

Even my discovery process was about "me" and "us"; it was rarely about "them."

'Continuity of service' implied that service had a starting point, but no end. This was the thought that changed the tide.

Listen, I wish I could tell you that I immediately went from 0-100, and I tripled my sales THAT year. It definitely didn't happen that way, so here's the deal.

What changed was my mindset, and therefore my language. Mentally, I went into meetings with the question, "What does service look like for this prospect?"

This question alone meant that I had to ask different questions, listen more completely (complete listening is something I'll address later), and develop a creativity that, up until this point, I'd lacked.

Losing a deal took on an entirely different meaning to me, as I began to think of the loss as yet another opportunity – not a lost opportunity, but an opportunity. My prospect-facing statement of 'let me know if anything changes,' morphed into the internal question. "How can I bring value to this prospect from this point until they either become a client or a source of clients in the future?"

"I'd love it if you'd use me as a resource."

Exchanging one dismissive statement for a veiled call to action, I began to get traction.

Initially, I was deathly afraid that telling folks to use me as a resource would result in a time suck with no real returns attached.

What if every prospect tried to use me for free information, free access to software, or something of the sort? How could I manage requests coming in from every angle while still trying to do my job?

Years later, I've not had such an occurrence and I've seen great results to boot.

Specificity has been key, however. I found that saying, "I'd love it if you'd use me as a resource" alone would leave the prospect without guidance on what that even means.

Once I started unpacking that for them, people would actually take me up on it, see the value in my service and solution, and several times they would boomerang to become clients.

Here's a real and practical example:

After several meetings and a couple of demos, I met with the VP of Tax at a large corporation. I was hoping to get the contract signed that day. All the I's had been dotted and T's crossed, at least in my estimation.

Upon my arrival, we exchange pleasantries and everything was going smoothly. In the midst of this, I state that based on our prior meetings, it seemed natural that we move forward unless there were other questions that had come up.

He looked at me and started, "Well....." Immediately I thought *"Houston, we have a problem."*

The VP began to explain to me his rationale for continuing with their current solution for another year. I let him know the reasons for my disagreement, reiterated to him the value that we'd uncovered during our times together, and ended with the unpacking I referred to earlier.

"I'd love it if you'd use me as a resource. Your team told me that comparative content between the 37 states you do business in is near-impossible to collect efficiently. Based on that, I want to serve you all. I'll send this to the team also, but please let me know when a project requires such a comparative. I'm more than happy to create that chart in real time and send it to you all.

I know that you also periodically deliver time-specific reports to the CFO around developments in the foreign countries you all have interests in. Let me help you there as well. Prior to your next CFO roundtable, let me know the date range you're presenting on, and which jurisdictions you're presenting in. I'll help supplement your research with a summary of all developments from those countries."

The VP now looks at me and says, "Wow, I really appreciate the offer." I look him in the eyes and respond, "No, I'm serious—no strings attached, I'd be excited to serve your organization in this way. If I don't hear from you in a couple weeks, I'll reach out to offer again. In addition, if I come across any content or events that I think would benefit you all, I'll send it your way."

Again, he responded with gratitude.

A week goes by, and I get an email from one of his tax managers that I'd never met with. "DeJuan, Stephen told us that you'd be willing to help us out from time to time. We're actually just starting a project dealing with CTC Reporting, and would like to compare what we're finding to what you guys have." He enumerated the 11 countries in question along with the specific topics, and within 15 minutes, I'd had a comparative chart built and sent over.

Along with that, I sent some special reports and news articles that I knew would matter to them.

A few days later, I get a call from the VP asking me if I'd be willing to come back in and do a demo with their International team. Apparently, the detail of the content I'd sent them went beyond what they could find anywhere else, and they were interested in what it would look like to add our international coverage to their current platform.

Spoiler alert: I went in and demoed to the International team. The response was overwhelming and the VP decided that instead of spending on two platforms, he'd consolidate spend, and simply replace their current solution with our full singular platform.

Service=Sales in this case.

It doesn't always turn out this easily this quickly, that much is true. There have been times that I would've needed to provide valuable content over the course of a year or more in order to acquire a new client.

Nevertheless, the point is three-fold.

1. Service should be the default setting for Sales Professionals.

2. Consistency in service builds value that can't be uncovered during discovery calls nor articulated in a pitch.

3. Commitment to service even after a "loss" is a powerful differentiator.

You may not be in an industry like the one I'm in, so this may look different for you.

Applying the three points above, however, **where could** you implement this approach in your business?

60.

I LOVE S.A.L.E.S.

By Phil Terrill

In my previous story, I introduced the 4F Model that helped me transform a dormant customer into a net-new win for Microsoft. However, I left out the story of the journey, effort and long back-and-forth discussion about digital transformation within an industry that was on the brink of severe disruption. Think of this as the "Amazon effect" in which anything that was a brick-and-mortar business needed to rethink how they planned to go to market in the future. At that time, one of my retail customers was really looking at how to evolve their company to match the frictionless way Amazon was targeting their customers. In reality, my customer was trying to figure out how to stay relevant enough for survival. That approach meant revamping their approach to investing in technology. Before I go too far, pay close attention to how I detail out this year-long engagement that developed with a really well-known global retailer in Southern California.

When I met this customer, they were moving down from a higher-tier segment within the company and required significant investment (or they perceived this as required treatment) based on their IT Manager's previous purchase in the region at another global retailer. However, this was my first meeting with the customer and it took a while to get it on the calendar. Let me give you a quick tip – account transitioning from the new fiscal year to the next appears seamless, but it is often the very opposite. In other words, prepare to be surprised by slow processes.

Once the account was transitioned, I quickly realized the influence the previous Account Manager had on the customer. My stakeholder was impressed with my ability to get a meeting put together so quickly, given name recognition was part of my territory optimization plan. On the podcast, I referenced being able to "humanize the relationship with technology" and that my first conversations with customers were hardly ever about just tech. My approach was to engage the new contact right where he was, because we actually started at our respective companies around the same time.

Doing critical research on your stakeholders is vital to the long-term success of any seller or person trying to make inroads with a new customer(s). Leverage social media and other platforms to understand your buyer, establish a persona, and feed those interests to ensure you are learning about the person behind the decision maker. When I realized his interests, we connected at varying levels, and this allowed me the opportunity to build a genuine connection. Our mutual interests in dogs, sports, good whiskey and the sun were always talking points. Just imagine if I could talk about LeBron going to the Lakers at that time.

After the connection was developed, I started to focus on providing valuable insights into the industry, access to in-market events, technical resources, and information on new technology that could improve their bottom line for IT (and beyond). The first step was gaining the relationship and now the focus became influence. The better the resource and timeliness of that value, the better off our discussions were about looking at other technology. I was able to steer the conversation towards a full portfolio review, leading to a conversation about how to optimize their investments so as to achieve the same functionality. At this point, it was critical to know my product/solution in order to present immediate value or advice that the customer could review to take action. This moment was critical because I knew that influence was established. We discussed areas they could divest or remove because the investment in a consolidated approach was extremely favorable to the company. In addition, we could reimagine how the company operationalized their retail footprint around the world.

To help the customer reach this destination, my first step was learning about the person who was going to make the decision. Every demo or proof-of-concept (POC) was a brick laid to help us get to the right foundation. My customer had tangible experiences and data at their fingertips to see the possibilities of a revamped technology roadmap. This included closing a three-year net-new deal inked at close to $1.8 million in total value to the customer. While a portion of that value was retired in quota, the impact in helping a customer achieve digital transformation was widely appreciated; the deployment against our roadmap has started making this a huge milestone for my initial stakeholder.

Even with this success, I am sure you are still wondering how this was really completed end-to-end. Well, some of that story is left out because the details might not be cool with Microsoft's legal team. However, I did want you to know what the S.A.L.E.S. acronym is all about, as these were the lessons I learned from collaborating with this retailer as their account executive:

Scale - **No one person alone can win the war!** Identify who is better than you and utilize their intelligence, expertise, and resources to help your customer(s).

Agility - Create a service level agreement (or SLA) with your customers that is realistic! Customers demand a lot, but you have to set expectations based on what you can actually deliver on time and at scale. There is a partnership that has to be established and **time is a finite resource**. Treat yours and theirs as such!

Leverage - My greatest successes in business, whether sales or not, **directly correlate to leveraging the incredible work and talents of others to create progress**. Progress is defined by business-value solutions, straight-forward results, and an undeniable appetite for excellence. The team won with our customers, because of leveraging each other in our best ways to be successful!

Experience - The best teacher of them all! **The only way to get results is to have skin in the game and just go for it**.

Otherwise, you might as well go do something else with your time. Michael Jordan said, "I can accept failure, but I cannot accept not trying" and that is an excellent perspective from arguably the greatest to ever do it in any sport!

Sacrifice - Success is about failing so fast that your next success makes you forget you ever failed in the first place. You have to be willing to go beyond the status quo for your customers! Bring them on the journey with you and it will be a different experience. Show them you are willing and able, but do it in a manner that exudes excellence. Be healthy and balanced in the process - no sale is worth dying over. Trust me on that one! Make that one extra call or type that one last email to a customer in order to increase the chances! The best are great because they do that little bit more than the others. **Greatness is a state of mind and not just a destination!**

The S.A.L.E.S. acronym is a framework that I still consider in my actions, as it provides key objectives or skills that I should constantly be driving towards with customers and partners. I hope you are able to utilize the stories to help you reach the 1% of performers. See you at the top!

CONCLUSION

You made it! What did you think? Which stories impacted you the most? Hopefully, you've already bookmarked them.

Reading and learning are great, but action is even better. What actions will you take now based on what you've read? Here are a few suggested actions to help you get more out of the time you've just invested and, hopefully, to get even more value from the other content and experiences I'll continue to work to curate for you.

Find an accountability partner or build a sales mastermind group. Read the book together. Talk about your biggest takeaways and what you will DO based on what you learned. Hold each other accountable and keep each other updated on your progress.

Subscribe to the Sales Success Stories Podcast. It's available anywhere and everywhere podcasts are found; if you'd like a set of direct links, go to top1.fm/Subscribe. Listen to the full interview with one or more of your favorite authors from the book and stay tuned for more to come. You'll find the episode numbers that each of the story contributors were featured in at the beginning of the book in the bios section.

If I'm doing things right, the most valuable thing you can do for yourself is to join the mailing list. If you go to top1.fm/BookReader, I've got some additional bonuses for you above and beyond what regular subscribers get. In addition to getting new episode updates and previews of future stories, which is the first place I share new opportunities, you'll find the very best offers regarding those opportunities.

What kinds of opportunities, you might ask? Right now we're planning two events per year - the Sales Success Summit and the President's

Club cruise. Both are all about the experience and exclusively feature the top 1% sales professionals from the podcast as they dig even deeper into the tips, tricks, and tactics they use for success in the real world. You'll also find details about future books and other content offerings.

When you join the mailing list, you'll immediately be given free access to at least three videos of your choice from the most recent Sales Success Summit and even more if you've also purchased the audio-book version!

Take a picture of yourself with the book. Share it on LinkedIn and tag me and your favorite authors along with some of your key takeaways.

Share your thoughts with me directly. You're welcome to email me: scott@top1.fm. If you have a question or a topic that you'd love to hear a real-world story about in a future book or podcast episode, I want to hear about it. Have your own story? Send it. I'm thinking about featuring some of those on top1.fm. Want to introduce me to the #1 seller at your company? Send me a note. You can also send inquiries about bulk purchase options if you want to buy copies of this book for your team, or perhaps you'd like to have me or another of the story contributors or podcast guests present at your next sales kick-off, quarterly business review, or another team meeting. Send me a note to talk about any of those.

Finally, if you enjoyed the book, please consider writing a short review wherever you purchased the book from. Your review will help someone else, like you, to find the book and make the decision to buy a copy for themselves.

Now go out there and get to work on creating your own Sales Success Story!

Made in the USA
Middletown, DE
04 November 2018